RESOURCEFUL LEADERSHIP

RESOURCEFUL LEADERSHIP

Tradeoffs and Tough Decisions
on the Road to School Improvement

—■—■—■—

ELIZABETH A. CITY

HARVARD EDUCATION PRESS
CAMBRIDGE, MASSACHUSETTS

Library of Congress Control Number 2007941436

Paperback ISBN 978-1-891792-86-1
Library Edition ISBN 978-1-891792-87-8

Published by Harvard Education Press,
an imprint of the Harvard Education Publishing Group

Harvard Education Press
8 Story Street
Cambridge, MA 02138

Cover Design: YAY! Design

The typefaces used in this book are Sabon for text and Adobe
Myriad Pro for display.

TO CHARLES E. LUCIER AND JUSTIN J. GREEN,

MY TEACHERS FIRST AND EVER

Contents

Foreword

Do resources matter? How much does it cost to create an excellent school? Does more spending lead to improved student performance? The relationship between spending and student performance confounds researchers, policymakers, and practitioners: Successful schools spend widely varying amounts per student, and statisticians struggle to find evidence of a strong relationship between dollars and results. Yet somehow it feels instinctively wrong that providing more resources wouldn't make education better.

Those who want to help schools improve have a hard time knowing how to respond when educators suggest that all they need is more money. This is because it matters very much *how* money is used—a point that Elizabeth City illustrates vividly in this book.

Over the last 15 years, I have worked with City and other colleagues at Education Resource Strategies (ERS) to explore how school leaders can make better use of the money they have. We have discovered that the first step toward making better use of dollars is to talk about "resources" instead. By resources we mean people first, time second, and dollars last. The second step is to use people, time, and dollars strategically to support student learning goals.

Schools that use resources strategically do three things:

1. Create a vision for what their school will accomplish
2. Define an instructional model that reflects that vision
3. *Organize* people, time, and money in ways that support it

Many school leaders do fairly well with the first two goals but falter when it comes to the "organizing" part of the effective resource use equation. This is not surprising, since the way we "do school" hasn't changed significantly in most of our lifetimes. Students are grouped by age and sometimes by subject. Teachers work independently, each with their own group of about 25 students. The school day lasts about seven hours, with the teachers' work day lasting slightly longer. The secondary school day is organized into six to seven periods, each devoted to a separate subject. Furthermore, the way schools get their resources—usually in the form of predefined staff positions whose number is determined based on specific class-size targets and a rigid model for the school schedule—does not encourage innovation, much less contemplation about how to best use people, time, or money.

What does it mean to organize resources to promote student learning? At ERS we use a framework based on years of research and study of how high-performing schools of all sizes and types organize their resources (Miles & Frank, 2008). While no school organizes resources in exactly the same way, high-performing schools organize people, time, and money to implement three "Guiding Resource Strategies":

1. They invest to continuously improve teaching quality through hiring, professional development, job structure, and common planning time.
2. They maximize academic time and link it to student learning needs.
3. They create individual attention and personal learning environments.

Schools follow common organizing principles to implement these strategies, but budgets, staffing, and schedules in effective schools can look very different, depending on a school's instructional model *and the resource context* (Shields & Miles, 2008). By resource context we mean how much money, expertise, and time a school has to work with and how much flexibility school leaders have to change the way each is used. Strategic school leaders account for this context by balancing resources to meet student needs.

In *Resourceful Leadership*, City allows us to follow two talented school leaders as they struggle to redesign their poorly performing schools using existing teachers and staff. Their challenges raise important issues for how districts can best support those who attempt to reverse declining schools, as well as for any leader seeking to create high-performing teacher teams. While these stories generate important lessons, they also inspire hope. As City describes, perhaps the most important resources are the intangible ones. At its heart, successful resource use is about the vision, hope, trust, energy, and ideas people bring to the task. In these pages, you will be treated to all five of these. City's special knack for attending closely to the daily reality of school life and making larger meaning of it ensures that readers will have a practical and inspiring experience.

Karen Hawley Miles
November 2007

REFERENCES

Miles, K. H., & Frank, S. (in press). *The strategic school: How to make the most of your school's people, time, and money.* Thousand Oaks, CA: Corwin Press.

Shields, R., & Miles, K. (in press). *Strategic designs: Lessons from leading-edge urban small high schools.* Boston: Education Resource Strategies.

Acknowledgments

Thanks first and foremost to the educators who participated in the study that is the foundation for this book. They gave generously of their time, a scarce resource in schools. Most particularly, I thank the principals—thoughtful, reflective practitioners who opened their practice in all its first-year messiness. To them all, I owe a huge learning debt. So many interviews with so many people left me inspired—it was a privilege to listen and learn. The work is hard and necessary and we are fortunate to have such good people doing it. Thank you.

This book draws heavily on the work of Education Resource Strategies (ERS). I am deeply indebted to my colleagues at ERS for helping me think about the connections between resources and schools that are great places for children and adults to learn. In particular, Karen Miles, Regis Shields, Nicole Ireland, and Julie Derderian contributed numerous insights and thoughtful conversations about interview protocols, data analysis, and findings that helped guide my work.

I am also grateful to my mentors and colleagues at the Harvard Graduate School of Education (HGSE), who have supported me in my development as a learner, leader, and scholar. While the people at HGSE who have contributed to my learning are too numerous to recount here, a few deserve special mention. Thanks to my dissertation committee, who supported this book from its first glimmer:

- My advisor, Robert Schwartz, who embodies Hope and Trust;
- Richard Murnane, who is a great teacher because he is a great learner;
- Richard Elmore, who embodies Vision with a relentless focus on instruction.

All of my committee members saw possibilities in me before I saw them and have helped me turn those into realities. In their daily work, they model how to continually connect high-quality research and high-quality practice.

A special thank you also to:

- Patricia Albjerg Graham, for continually urging me to focus on what counts—especially when it's not countable
- Susan Moore Johnson, for encouraging me to find my voice and for teaching me how to listen as a researcher
- Sarah Fiarman, Sara Suchman, Folashade Cromwell, and Simone Sangster, for supremely helpful reading of drafts and much-less-than-drafts.

I also gratefully acknowledge funding support from the Herold Hunt Fellowship, Achievement Gap Initiative Dissertation Research Fellowship, and the Spencer Research Training Grant, which made it possible for me to devote the time and attention needed to listen, learn, and write. The Bill & Melinda Gates Foundation supported much of the data collection through my work with ERS.

I extend my gratitude to the numerous educator colleagues in Boston, Cambridge, and beyond who checked on my writing progress, encouraged me, and told me I would finish. We all need cheerleaders and accountants. Thank you for being both.

This book would not be in your hands without the commitment and talent of many people at Harvard Education Press. My thanks to all of you, with particular appreciation for Caroline Chauncey, who has just the right combination of encouragement, nudging, and insight. I also gratefully acknowledge the anonymous reviewers who supplied thoughtful feedback. The book is better because of you.

Finally and fundamentally, a special thanks to my family, whose unconditional love and support is my most precious resource.

—■—■—■—

Introduction

"Everything that can be counted isn't worth counting, and
everything that is worth counting isn't always countable."
                                                  —*Albert Einstein*

There's a lot of counting going on in American schools these days.
What progress are we making toward the professed—and historically unprecedented—national goal of all students reaching proficiency by 2014? The 2007 National Assessment of Education Progress
(NAEP) shows that we are closer to this goal today than at any point
in the 30+ year history of the test (Lee, Grigg, & Donahue, 2007; Lee,
Grigg & Dion, 2007). The most dramatic improvements have been in
math, with the percentage of students at or above Proficient tripling for
fourth graders and doubling for eighth graders from 1990 to 2007.

But we are still far from the goal of 100 percent proficiency. Even with
steady improvement, only one-third of fourth and eighth graders are
Proficient in reading. Fourth graders fare slightly better in math, with
39 percent Proficient, while about one-third of eighth graders are Proficient. The news is worse at the high school level, where the percentage
of seniors performing at or above Proficient in reading dropped from 40
percent in 1992 to 35 percent in 2005 (Grigg, Donahue, & Dion, 2007).
Less than one-quarter of seniors scored at or above Proficient in math-

ematics. Even within individual states, where measures of proficiency differ (and are usually less stringent) than NAEP, we are not close to *all* students being Proficient in reading and math.

We are farthest from this goal with the students our schools have historically served least well, including poor students, students with disabilities, and students of color. The good news is that the performance trend is generally upward for all groups of students. The bad news is that gaps persist, with appalling manifestations, like African American and Latino high school seniors scoring on average at the same level in math and reading as the average white eighth grader. And that only speaks to the students who stay in school until their senior year, which many students do not. The national graduation rate is around 71 percent, and is markedly worse for African American (56%) and Latino students (54%) (Greene, 2002)[1].

Better than ever is not good enough.

One solution to the challenge of helping all students reach proficiency has been to pour more resources into schools. In the three decades since NAEP began taking the performance temperature of our schools, per pupil spending has doubled, after adjusting for inflation (National Center for Education Statistics, 2005). No Child Left Behind has emphasized getting "highly-qualified" teachers into every classroom, and districts and schools have spent time improving the knowledge and skill of teachers through professional development.

Recently, high schools have been the target of much attention. As many researchers and policymakers have noted, the American high school is largely unchanged from the 1920s and is particularly entrenched in history and popular imagination, with several expected characteristics such as extracurricular activities, a thick catalog of courses, and tracks for the college-bound and not-college-bound (Tyack and Cuban, 1995; Sizer, 1984; Powell, Farrar, & Cohen, 1985). In response to this inertia, the federal government and private foundations like the Carnegie Corporation and the Bill & Melinda Gates Foundation have invested hundreds of millions of dollars in high school redesign.

Mounting evidence suggests that at all levels of schooling, more resources and structural solutions such as size are not enough—schools are not necessarily going to serve students better just because they're small or spend more money. They have to do things differently. What are those things, and what does it look like to try to do them in a context where urgency and accountability outstrip knowledge about improvement? What needs to happen in schools to maximize the likelihood that they can and will take actions that improve student outcomes? How do schools do that with scarce resources?

This book takes on these questions, with a particular focus on the multiple decisions that school leaders make about resources. The work is not easy. Even with smart, dedicated people, we don't always improve as fast and as much as we would like. This book is about why it's hard and what to do to make your efforts and investments more effective—and hopefully a little easier.

A BRIEF OVERVIEW OF THE BOOK

Armed with a list of over 200 quantifiable indicators of resource use, I headed into schools to collect data and report on how the schools used their resources of people, time, and money. I should have known better. Very little of my own experience working in schools as a teacher, coach, or principal can be captured in numbers. Schools are stories because schools are fundamentally about people. I knew this well enough to know that I should talk with people as I collected my numbers, but I still thought the numbers would carry most of the story.

I was wrong. As I analyzed the budgets and the schedules and listened to principals, administrators, teachers, students, and district personnel, the story that emerged was not so much about resources as it was about change. People, time, and money mattered, but there were other elements not on my list of quantifiable indicators that kept cropping up. Those elements were vision, hope, trust, ideas, and energy, and they seemed to matter at least as much as people, time, and money and to affect the use of those resources.

This book synthesizes what I learned with what is more broadly known about resource use in schools. The book is for leaders who want to be "resourceful"—leaders who want to use resources creatively and strategically to make decisions that support improvement. It is also for the district personnel, external partners, university educators, and policymakers who want to support resourceful school leaders. The book aims to help you understand why investments in schools don't always work as planned, and how to think about which investments make sense for improvement.

Chapter 1 offers an overview of what the limited research tells us about resource uses that make a difference for student achievement. For the most part, what you would expect to matter usually does, like good teaching (Haycock, 1998). But some of our assumptions about what matters may not be wholly supported by evidence (e.g., teachers with more education are more effective), and some things may not be what we'd expect (e.g., smaller class sizes are not unequivocally a good choice if you want higher student achievement). The chapter offers guidelines for how to navigate the murky waters of what is "known" about effective resource use.

Chapter 2 defines vision, hope, trust, ideas, and energy and offers examples of what they look like and why they might matter. What are the roots of resistance? How can doing the "right" things sometimes be so wrong? How does a writing contest change a teacher's mind about what students can do? And how can school leaders cultivate the roots that will support growth?

Chapters 3, 4, and 5 examine the resources of people, time, and money. The separation of those resources into distinct chapters is a bit artificial since they overlap, but there are particular levers and decisions for each resource. Chapter 3 looks at hiring, professional development, and supervision and evaluation as opportunities with people. This chapter zooms in on coaching as one promising but challenging practice. Chapter 4 investigates two dimensions of time: organizing it and using it to provide individual attention, including the challenge of personalizing learning so that *all* students reach proficiency and maximize their potential. Chapter 5 addresses the topic of money. As the most publicly-discussed resource, its late position in the book may come as a surprise. That sequencing will make sense when you get to it, as will the fact that it's the shortest resource chapter.

Chapter 6 looks at the complex role of the district as both help and hindrance for schools. The chapter explores how districts can use strategy, precision, personalization, and relationships to do the very things for schools that they want schools to do for children.

The book's conclusion addresses the question of "so what?" What are the major takeaways for school leaders and the people who support them? The appendices include recommended resources, considerations when scheduling, and some of the quantifiable resource indicators for the schools involved in the study.

A TALE OF TWO SCHOOLS, TWO SCHOOL LEADERS, AND THE CHALLENGE OF CHANGE

To be helpful, this book needs to offer frameworks for thinking about the multiple decisions school leaders make. It does that, but if it did only that, it would be dreadfully dull. It would also miss the point, which is that decisions do not happen in a vacuum. They are part of a complex context that affects whether decisions are likely or unlikely to generate the intended outcomes.

For context, this book takes two real schools in the midst of great change—their first year as small high schools that have been converted from a large, comprehensive high school. This context offers two important learning opportunities:

1. Amplifying the many decisions that school leaders make because these leaders are making them for the first time. In other words, decisions that are not so obvious when studying existing schools— you have a schedule; why does it look the way it does?—are easier to see and explore when leaders are in the process of making their original decision rather than revising an existing decision. This is helpful for exposing the complexity of leaders' decisionmaking processes, as well as for articulating the factors they considered when making decisions.
2. Examining the connections between change and resource use. What does it look like to undergo significant change? What are the impli-

cations for resource use, particularly resource use that will lead to improvement in student outcomes?

The tale of these two schools and the two principals who lead them is woven throughout the book. In order to delve deeply and develop a rich picture of the nuances of resource use, I limited my study to two schools, which has the inevitable trade-off of breadth and generalizability. Some elements of the tale will be particular to these schools and these principals, or more applicable to high schools than elementary schools, small schools than large schools, urban schools than nonurban schools. But I suspect that you will see elements of the challenges and decisions you face if you are trying to improve schools, no matter what size they are, where they are, or the age of the students they serve.

Tech High and Health High

The two schools, which I call Tech High and Health High (names of people, schools, and the district have been changed for confidentiality), are similar to many other urban public high schools in terms of their student demographics, student achievement, and resource levels (see Appendix for details). At the time of this study, in 2005–2006, the schools were two of four small schools that had just been converted from the same 1300-student high school, Darby Comprehensive High School (DCHS). Many of their teachers and students were part of DCHS previously and now shared the same building. The schools also shared the context of being in a midsized urban district ("Metro Public School District") that saw small high schools as part of its high school reform strategy, and they operated within the same district policies and union regulations.

The boxy exterior of the DCHS building gives few clues about the architectural maze that is the interior. The building spans five floors, connected by multiple staircases and hallways that don't always begin and end in intuitive places. Traversing the building requires choosing the right combination of doorways and stairwells, a task made more complicated by the division of the building into four schools. Each school sits in a particular region of the school—Tech High mostly on the west side, fourth floor; Health High mostly on the east side, third floor—but both schools have classrooms on at least three floors, not including the centrally-located cafeteria, gym, and library, which are shared by all four small schools. Students are supposed to stay in their school's space.

Many of the teachers and administrators at Darby had been there since the school was built in the 1970s, and had a long history of contributing to Darby's comprehensive curricular and extracurricular offerings and to its reputation as one of the most sought-after high schools in the district. Metro Public School District (MPSD) decided that popularity and comparatively good test scores were not sufficient reasons to leave DCHS intact when the goal was proficiency for all. This opinion was not shared by DCHS administrators, teachers, and students, who initially opposed the conversion of DCHS into four small schools, but later participated in a process of designing what the new schools would look like.

Tony Hobbs and Paula Martin

For both Tony Hobbs and Paula Martin the new schools were the site of their first principalship. Both principals were people of color, were devoted to improving outcomes for urban students, and had a comfortable, respectful rapport with students. They had prior experience with efficient resource use at the level of both practice and theory, including studying with Karen Hawley Miles, a leading researcher and consultant to urban districts about resource use.

Tony Hobbs, the principal of Tech High, was one of the youngest principals in the district. He had teaching and administrative experience at another small high school in the district that used resources strategically and was one of the district's highest performing high schools. He had a vision for what a small school looked like and great optimism about the possibilities for teachers' and students' success.

Paula Martin, the principal of Health High, had come to education and the principalship as a second career after a career in public health. She brought with her managerial experience and ideas about resource use from a different sector. As a longtime parent and resident in MPSD, Martin felt great urgency in getting better opportunities and results for students.

Both principals knew a lot about resource use, were in schools with relatively high resource levels, and were in a district that wanted to support them. And yet both principals struggled. The book follows them through their first year, not marching through the school calendar, but relaying their experiences within a framework for thinking about resourceful leadership.

The Challenge of Change

This book shows the messiness of real schools and real school leaders trying to make decisions that are ultimately good for kids. It shows why this process is so hard and what school leaders can do to turn change into improvement.

The work of improvement is incredibly difficult. Even when you know how to use resources well, the work is difficult because you are trying to convert not a building, but beliefs and practices. Drawing on research-based notions of effective resource use can help, but you have to mobilize resources to work together, you have to expand your notion of "resources," and you have to constantly make decisions and assess whether those decisions are working.

Numbers only tell part of the story. This is not to say that numbers aren't worth something. They are. But they are not everything. The recent trend to "count" in education is long overdue. It's part of a broader conversation to agree on what matters, what our schools should be doing, and for whom. The limitation is not with the idea of agreeing on what matters, but in our own capacity to envision multiple ways of understanding whether we're accomplishing what we want to accomplish. A lack of imagination, we might call it. Just as we cannot blame students for falling short of our learning goals if we do not provide the schools and instruction they need to attain those goals, we cannot blame the goals if we do not provide the means for "measuring" them, whether by numbers or words or pictures or some yet unimagined means. Examining resources reinforces this tendency to count what is countable.

In the end, the story in all our schools is a story with both words and numbers, with both countables and uncountables. In this book, you will hear the story about one urban school of 1,300 students becoming 4 schools of 300–400 students. Some characters in the story call it a "conversion," some call it a "transformation," and some call it a "dismantling." Some of the words connote a more positive spin than others, but they all speak of significant change.

Here, then, is my attempt to describe resource use in the midst of change. Some of it is countable, and some of it is not. It is all worth counting.

CHAPTER ONE

—■—■—■—

Resource Use
That Counts

Ask parents whether they would prefer to send their children to schools with more resources, ask teachers whether they would prefer to have smaller class sizes, ask principals whether they would prefer to have more time in the school day or year, and you will probably hear a resounding "yes." Yet research suggests that none of these options—more resources, smaller class sizes, more time—consistently makes a difference in student achievement. Other choices that pass the "common sense" test (of course more money would be better!) often fail to produce evidence that they matter for student outcomes, including professional development for teachers and hiring teachers with more education.

So what are we to do? We want to improve outcomes for students, our best instincts tell us that resources must matter somehow, but research suggests we should mostly look elsewhere for the magic keys that will unlock the doors to student success.

Before we throw up our hands, default to our preferred take on resource use, and search elsewhere for those magic keys, we should pause. Dissonance between instinct and research doesn't mean that we know nothing. It means we know some things, many of them contradictory, and that we need to explore the subject a bit more.

My reading of the research, combined with my own experience as an educator, suggests that there aren't magic resource keys, but there are keystones that can help, each with implications for action. These basic principles are:

1. Quantity matters some—but *quality* matters more;
2. We know more—and less—than we think we do;
3. Resource use matters, but people, time, and money are not enough.

The first of these is the most critical, and thus will get the most attention in this chapter, followed by a brief examination of the other two keystones.

QUANTITY MATTERS SOME—BUT *QUALITY* MATTERS MORE

More dollars, small class size, and more time can contribute to a difference in student outcomes. What matters most, however, is how resources are used. Additional resources probably won't help improve outcomes if teaching and learning look the same as they did in rooms with fewer dollars, more students, and less time. But more resources just might help if they are used purposefully to change the teaching and learning happening in classrooms. Quantity matters some, but *quality* matters more.

A closer look at the ways in which people, time, and money are used illustrates the principle of quality over quantity, and shows what quality looks like.[1]

People

Teaching matters for learning. In fact, some research suggests that it is teaching that matters most for student achievement (Sanders and Rivers, 1996; Rivkin, Hanushek, & Kain, 2005). The resource of people is thus the most precious resource in schools. How do we get the best teachers? Through hiring, supervision and evaluation, and professional development.

Schools can influence teaching quality through whom they hire and how. Case studies show that high-performing schools carefully evaluate potential employees and hire to fit the school's design and needs (Miles & Darling-Hammond, 1998; Center for Collaborative Education, 2001; Darling-Hammond, Ancess, & Ort, 2002; Education Resource Strategies, forthcoming). The hiring process matters, too. New teachers who report that the hiring process gave them an accurate picture of their job also report being more satisfied in their job than teachers who did not see the hiring process as information-rich (Liu, 2004). This focus on hiring is consistent with the noneducation literature. In a study of highly effective companies, Collins and colleagues found that "getting the right people on the bus" was a key component that differentiated "great" companies from "good" ones (2001).

The evidence is mixed on the significance of teacher education level or content preparation (Hanushek, 1997; Thompson, 1998; Wayne & Youngs, 2003), though college course work in the content area being taught is an indicator of teacher quality for math and science teachers at the high school level (Goldhaber & Brewer, 1997, 1998, 2000; Goldhaber & Anthony, 2003). The evidence is less clear for other subject areas and grade levels, which suggests that getting high-quality teachers is more complicated than hiring people with the most education or highest test scores.

Given the difficulty of predicting at the point of hiring how effective teachers will be, researchers Gordon, Kane, and Staiger recommend that more attention be paid to keeping effective teachers and not keeping ineffective teachers (2006), a notion that is more radical in many schools and districts than it might sound. To improve average teacher effectiveness, they recommend that least effective teachers not be promoted to tenure-track positions, and that the effectiveness of teachers be assessed through student achievement and evaluations by principals, peers, and parents. Their recommendation is buoyed by the evidence that principals can correctly identify their most effective and least effective teachers in terms of student achievement (Jacob & Lefgren, 2005). While there is little proof that formal evaluation results in improved student achievement, research suggests that ongoing feedback on teaching may be associated with more effective teachers and schools, and that feedback is not necessarily provided by a principal (Elmore, 2004; Rosenholtz, 1985; Natriello, 1984).

In addition to getting the right people on and off the bus, a primary strategy for influencing teaching quality is providing professional development and support. American schools invest billions of dollars in professional development. However, there is little evidence that most of this investment makes a difference in student achievement, in part because it is hard to tease out the effect of professional development from other factors. But the dearth of evidence can also be explained by the quality of the professional development, which in many cases doesn't support either adult or student learning.

In the area of professional development, the few available statistical studies point to the importance of its being content-focused, coherent, and frequent in order to make a difference in teacher effectiveness (Cohen & Hill, 2001; Jacob & Lefgren, 2002; Holcombe, 2002). Multiple studies highlight the importance of teachers working collaboratively around student work and instruction (e.g., Elmore, 2004; Hargreaves, 1994; Miles & Darling-Hammond, 1998).[2] Here again, the focus is on quality—what are teachers doing during professional development time?

Time

For many educators, time is the scarcest resource, and not one over which it seems they have control. But time, like other resources, can be managed, and when managed in particular ways, contributes to improved student achievement. There are two primary dimensions of time as a resource: organizing it (which includes scheduling), and using it to provide individual attention for students.

Schools that devote more time and longer blocks of time to literacy and math and *use this time well* have improved student achievement (Education Trust, 1999; Lake, Hill, O'Toole, & Celio, 1999). In other words, more time is better, with the key caveat that it matters a lot how that time is used. More time on bad instruction doesn't help. The research on the effectiveness of longer blocks of instructional time in high schools shows mixed effects, but suggests that blocks are unlikely to be effective unless accompanied by support for teachers in learning to make use of the time (Rice, Croninger, & Roellke, 2002; Marchant & Paulson, 2001; Veal & Flinders, 2001; Zapeda & Mayers, 2001).[3]

The ratio of teacher time to student time is another aspect that needs to be examined. A recent case study showed that high-performing schools tended to have higher ratios of teacher time to student time than comparison schools within their districts (Education Resource Strategies, forthcoming). In other words, teachers in high-performing schools spent considerably more time in the schools than the students, whereas in other schools teacher time and student time tended to be similar (for example, in many schools, teachers arrive 15 minutes before and leave 15 minutes after students). Again, this does not mean that simply adding more time for teachers makes schools high performing. It matters what schools do with that additional time, and schools that have longer days for teachers may also attract different kinds of teachers from schools that don't.

A number of practices make it possible for students to receive more individualized attention, including assessments, support and enrichment, and teacher load. Assessments are one strategy for identifying what students know and can do, which then makes it possible to respond to individual students' needs. High-performing and improving classrooms and schools integrate assessments into the everyday life of the school and use ongoing assessments to inform instruction and school decisions (Black & Wiliam, 1998; Springboard Schools, 2003). This aligns with common sense—it's much easier to make targeted and effective improvements if you know what's already working and what needs improving.

A necessary corollary to using assessments is responding to them with appropriate support and enrichment. The limited available research suggests that high-performing schools do so, including tutoring and extra time for struggling students (Darling-Hammond, Ancess, & Ort, 2002; Hock, Pulver, Deshler, & Schumaker, 2001), often imbedding support (both academic and social/emotional) within the school day (Education Resource Strategies, forthcoming).

An increasingly popular strategy for support and enrichment time in high schools is the use of advisories in which small groups of students (typical size: 13–18 students) meet regularly with an adult (the "advisor," who is a teacher or administrator). Advisories usually meet for 20–30 minutes, anywhere from once a week to daily. While the content varies across schools (academic, social/emotional, college/career planning), the theory is consistent, which is that students will have more success if they have a relationship with at least one adult in the building and if one adult is paying close attention to them. Though the use of advisories in high schools is increasingly widespread, the limited available evidence about their effectiveness is mixed, and suggests again that quality matters.[4]

While common sense suggests that teachers might be able to give more attention to individual students if they had fewer students, research offers little data in the area of teacher load (i.e., how many students a teacher instructs). One recent study found that reduced teacher loads helped a high school reach the highest level of school performance for schools under the district's school accountability plan (Archibald, 2001). Another recent study found that some high-performing high schools had reduced teacher loads (17–75 students/teacher), while others had more typical high school teacher loads (125–150), and used structures like looping (teachers staying with the same students for more than one year) to know students well (Education Resource Strategies, forthcoming). Here again, a resource structure might support the potential for a higher-quality learning experience for students, but it neither ensures nor provides the exclusive pathway to quality.

Money

Research on money focuses primarily on *effectiveness*—what's the relationship between money and student achievement outcomes? and *adequacy*—is there enough money to achieve the desired outcomes? Neither area is particularly illuminating, primarily because, as in other resource areas, it matters greatly how the money is spent, a notion supported by the preponderance of evidence that more money doesn't necessarily mean better student achievement (Hanushek, 1997; Hedges, Laine, & Greenwald, 1994; Ladd & Hansen, 1999).

Many of the ways in which money can matter have already been described in the People and Time sections of this chapter. In this section, we look at two more dimensions of money—one, as an additional resource in the form of external funds and partnerships, and the other, a popular and expensive target of money—reduced class size.

Though there is scant research on the role of external funds and partnerships in student performance, some case studies suggest that high-performing schools draw on external funds and resources, such as community and college resources, to provide additional courses, opportunities, and services for students (Center for Collaborative Education, 2001; Education Resource Strategies, forthcoming). A key feature of external funds cited by principals is not the amount of money (though few principals turn up their noses at any sum of money), but the *flexibility* to spend the money according to the needs they identified.

Reducing class size is a popular and expensive strategy that schools and districts deploy to improve student performance. Some class size research suggests that reductions in class size might make a small difference in student achievement at the early elementary level (Hanushek, 1998), while other research suggests that improved achievement outcomes depend on teachers changing their instruction (Finn, Gerber, Achilles, & Boyd-Zaharias, 2001; Mishel & Rothstein, 2002). A few small-scale studies suggest that high-performing high schools have smaller class sizes, but more research is needed to see whether there is a causal link between class size and student performance at the high school level (Archibald, 2001; Darling-Hammond, Ancess, & Ort, 2002; Deutsch, 2003; Education Resource Strategies, forthcoming).

The implication for education leaders is to focus on quality. Quantity might help, but only if you use it well.

WE KNOW MORE—AND LESS—THAN WE THINK WE DO

The soundscape of knowledge about what works in schools is often discordant, rarely harmonious. This is even more true in the area of resources than in some other areas of education. There is a dearth of research about resource use, particularly research that draws a causal link between resource use and student outcomes. The limited literature looks at existing high-performing schools and their resource use, but does not describe how the schools got to be high-performing—was it through using resources in particular ways, or is the observed resource use an indicator of something else that is driving the high performance?

The soundscape is particularly sparse at the high school level, where students have multiple teachers and peer groups, and there are fewer available measures of achievement, thereby complicating the already-difficult task of causally connecting resources and achievement. The difficulty of following the chain of cause and effect from a particular resource use to improved instruction to improved student achievement when there are many other factors at play contributes to both the scarcity and the disharmony of available evidence. Where there is research, it can appear to contradict other research or our own instincts and experience—class size *must* matter, right?

Dissonance and scarcity do not, however, give us license to tune in only to whatever resonates with us. We, and more important, students, lose out if we say that there's not enough quality research, so better to rely on instinct and experience; or if we say that instinct and experience are too anecdotal and unsupported by research, so better to rely on the narrow band of research that does exist. Truth is not that simple. We know more—and less—than we think we do.

We know more than is confirmed by solid research, and we know it through common sense and lived experience. But what we think we know is not always right, particularly beyond the context in which we think we know it. Our best bet is to ask questions and listen carefully, especially to students, an oft-overlooked source of valuable information about both quality and effectiveness. Students can tell you when class time is used well and when it is not. Students can tell you whether they are getting the support they need to be successful. If you ask them, students will also tell you that they want more PE (as some do at Health High), and that they wish they could eat and play football outside during lunch (as some do at Tech High). Such sentiments may sound as if students are not serious about their studies, but their desire to move more is supported by brain research that connects movement to learning.[5]

The implication for school leaders is to listen actively and openly to multiple sources of information and inspiration—instinct, experience, research, and resource consumers—and to base decisionmaking on the combination of what you learn.

RESOURCE USE MATTERS, BUT PEOPLE, TIME, AND MONEY ARE NOT ENOUGH

The final keystone is both reassuring and challenging. While it's helpful to know that high-quality use of people, time, and money can support student learning, it's not easy to know which resource levers to pull. Leading researchers and practitioners in the area of resources assert that using resources "strategically," or in ways that research would suggest are effective and make sense for what the school or district is trying to do given their context, can catalyze improvement, particularly by creating the structural conditions for high performance (Miles & Frank, forthcoming; Miles, 2001; Odden & Archibald, 2001; Darling-Hammond, Ancess, & Ort, 2002). In other words, resource use drives improvement. Much of the school reform/change literature includes some reference to resources, particularly the idea of aligning resources with the goals of the reform so that resources are targeted at the reform rather than fragmented across multiple areas (Newmann, Smith, Allensworth, & Bryk, 2001; Fullan, 2001). In other words, improvement drives resource use. Whichever way you look at it, resources are a necessary but not sufficient component of improvement.

Though research suggests that ongoing assessment and adjustment of resource use is a feature of high-performing schools (Education Resource Strategies, forthcoming), research offers little to suggest how resource use directly connects to improvement and how it might consequently vary over time—for example, how might resource use look different at different points in the improvement process, or in different schools depending on the schools' capacity for improvement? Some of the resource literature discusses the importance of articulating an instructional vision before organizing resources to support that vision (e.g., Odden & Archibald, 2001), but there is little explicit discussion of the resource use required to enable a school to articulate an instructional vision.

Some of the broader literature points in the direction of factors less tangible than people, time, or money that may also be considered resources. For instance, a clear, articulated vision is widely recognized as a feature of high-performing schools and as a key to improvement (Fullan, 2001; Hallinger & Heck, 1996; Springboard Schools, 2003; Hawley, 2002). Research also suggests that educators' view of their role in change makes a difference for improvement. When teachers and principals believe that what they do matters, a school is more likely to be improving (Elmore, 2004; Dembo & Gibson, 1985).

Trust is another key element of improvement. In fact, researchers Bryk and Schneider name "trust" as a "core resource for improvement" (2002, book title). In their study of Chicago elementary schools engaged in reform, they found that schools that were improving on "relational trust," which they characterized as "respect, competence, personal regard for others, and integrity," had more significant improvements in student achievement than schools that were not improving on relational trust (2002). The authors' approach was unconventional in that it measured the improvement of the "resource" (trust) and how it connected to the improvement of student achievement. The limited research that links resources and improvement tends to look at resources as static and student achievement as the focus of measuring "improvement," which oversimplifies the improvement process.

The implication for school leaders is to embrace complexity while focusing on quality and listening actively and openly, all while considering people, time, and money as one piece in the improvement puzzle. That's easier preached than practiced, as we'll see in the remaining chapters. During the first year at Tech High and Health High, several elements surfaced as critical for improvement, and as directly tied to the efficient and effective use of people, time, and money.

—■—■—■—

CHAPTER TWO

Vision, Hope, Trust, Ideas, and Energy

"The only thing that's changed from last year to this year is me. It's the same kids. It's the same teachers teaching the same things. That doesn't change overnight. Where do I start with my algebra teacher upstairs?"

—Principal Hobbs, Tech High

"You're charged with making change and doing things differently, but you're given a faculty that doesn't share any of that. They don't share the need. They don't think there was a problem at all, even when you show them the data. They don't think there was a problem with the teaching that was going on, with the instruction, or the way things were organized. They think there was a problem with the kids who came to school."

—Principal Martin, Health High

C hange. Both principals speak of it, want it, invest in it. Most of their faculty and students hear it, don't want it, resist it. The work of change is hard. The work of improvement is harder. This chapter is about what makes the work hard, and about why we do it. It is about what you need to invest in to create the conditions for wise decision-making about people, time, and money. It is about the elements of improvement that are not easily counted, but are worth counting: vision, hope, trust, ideas, and energy. Of all the scarce assets in schools, these are perhaps the scarcest, and the hardest to quantify.

As we will see in subsequent chapters, both principals Martin and Hobbs did many things "right" with their resources of time, people, and money. They did many of the things research suggests will lead to better outcomes for students. But they also did many things "wrong." They invested money and people and time into efforts that yielded no improvement in teacher practice or student learning. The trouble is the "right" things and "wrong" things can be the same things. For example, research would suggest that coaching is a good use of resources for instructional improvement. Each school spent about $125,000 on coaching. By all accounts, only a small fraction of that made any difference in teacher practice or student learning.

It was a waste because both schools invested poorly given their circumstances: they were in the initial phases of significant change and there was little commonly held belief about the need for change, much less what that change should look like. Most of the resources that were poured into making the change happen were wasted because neither the adults nor the students in the schools were ready for change. As these two new small high schools show, vision, hope, trust, ideas, and energy are where the focus needs to be in the first year of a big change in order to create the conditions needed for improvement.

This chapter is purposely not called "culture," which is bandied about in education as a catchall for the things we can't name and describe, but we know are important. My work in schools has shown me that the more precise we can be with words, the easier it is to establish a common language and shared understanding, which are essential ingredients for improvement. Thus, I've named the specific aspects of what matters in these two schools as they try both to change and to improve. Even at a level of generality, "culture" is not quite the right word for what mattered in these two new schools. "Culture" connotes something that is in the air everywhere. The aspects I describe here are everywhere, but they are better described as roots—largely invisible at a surface glance, essential before we can see growth in other places, and interconnected. "Cultivation" is a more apt word than culture because it describes the intentional attention that roots (and culture) require to grow.

This chapter introduces the five roots that mattered most in these two new schools in their first year and provides examples of each. They will appear again in the remaining chapters.

VISION

Principal Hobbs and Principal Martin each had a vision that drove their decisions, but that vision was not clearly articulated. That invisibility made things harder. Four elements of vision were critical at Tech High and Health High:

- Purpose and expectations (what you're trying to do/achieve)
- Core values (deeply held beliefs and sense of what's important)
- Theory of action (ideas about how you achieve a desired outcome—if we do x, then y will happen)
- Need for change (when the above elements aren't being met, people in the schools see the need for change)

Purpose and Expectations

At Health High, Principal Martin discovered that her vision of a "health" school was quite different from that of her faculty. Many teachers signed on to the school thinking that it would be an "eat well and exercise school," and were interested in it because of their personal experiences with Weight Watchers. Martin, on the other hand, thought being a health school was about giving students a solid science and math foundation so that they could pursue a variety of health careers. Martin's vision was more oriented to what students would be able to do after they finished high school, while her teachers were more focused on what the high school experience would be for students. For Martin, the high school experience was a means to another end—successful college attendance and a career—not the end in itself, which meant she wasn't content with students eating well and exercising. Neither the faculty nor the students protested when Martin told them that she was raising the graduation requirements. Students at Health High would be required to pass 4 years of math and 4 years of science. In the district, students had to take 4 years of math, but only had to pass 3 (a gap that Martin interpreted as the city saying it was okay to fail a year of math), and had to take and pass 3 years of science. No one outwardly disagreed with Martin, but that did not mean that they shared a vision. The lack of dissension about raising the requirements was in part because some people agreed with Martin that it was good to raise the bar, others deferred to her experience about what was needed for health careers, and others found it hard to argue against "high expectations," a popular mantra in urban schools. That didn't mean, however, that everyone embraced, or even understood, Martin's vision of rigorous academic preparation.

A more subtle expectation that separated Martin from her faculty and her students was her expectation that students would succeed, and her definition of "success." At Darby Comprehensive High School, the faculty and students generally accepted the fact that some students applied to college and others didn't, and it was good enough that the school had the highest college application rate for nonexam/magnet schools in the district. For Martin, this was not good enough. Her goal was that all students would apply and get in and have the option to attend at least one college, preferably a four-year college. She had no experience with college applications beyond her own children, but she was determined to figure it out. Her guidance counselor was not helpful. The guidance counselor told one student he could not get on the bus for a college visit because his grades were too low. Martin told the counselor, "That's ridiculous. If he wants to go look at the college, let him go look at the college." Martin wrote all the students' recommendations because she did not trust the counselor to pitch them well.

The primary obstacle, however, was getting students to apply at all. Martin summarized students' resistance: "I think a lot of them don't apply because they don't think they're going to get in, and they'd rather not experience the failure. It's so much easier to just not take a risk on all this. And their grades are horrible. They've never done well in school. And so they're like, 'No, I'm not doing this. I'm not experiencing another failure.' " Martin cajoled and supported students individually in the application process. Eventually, every senior but one (who had already signed up for hairdressing school) applied to college, and all were accepted to at least one college.

The gap between Martin's expectations and her faculty's and students' expectations led to great inefficiencies, including the vast amounts of time that Martin devoted to college applications and the $88,000[1] spent on paying the guidance counselor for a job that Martin was doing most of herself. The plus side was that once a few students were accepted to colleges, it was easier to convince other students to apply. One student described this seeing as believing phenomenon as "If they can go, I can go, too." The minus side was that the guidance counselor had not changed her practices at all, so additional resources would need to be devoted to the college application process the following year.

Core Values

The multiple views of purpose and expectations in play at both schools were informed by different sets of core values—the deeply held beliefs and feelings of what was important. Hobbs and Martin quickly learned that many of their teachers' core values about the students in their schools and the adults' responsibility for them differed from theirs. In the summer before Tech High opened, Hobbs worked with his teachers on advisory, which he knew was a new and foreign concept to most of them. As the faculty worked on advisory, one teacher expressed an approach to teaching of "dropping stuff off at the dock for students." The teacher had done his job by delivering it, and it was up to students to pick it up or not, their choice. In another advisory-related activity, the faculty did a word storm around the word "student" and came up with words like "customer," "mean," and "delinquent." It became clear to Hobbs that the faculty needed to have lots of conversations to chip away at these notions of students and the role of the adults in the school toward students.

Only four months into the school year, Martin was past thinking that conversation would bridge the chasm between her beliefs and values and those of many of her teachers: "I don't really like having a team of people that don't really believe the same way you do. I find it really, really disheartening. I also no longer believe that you try to build consensus around the vision and the values. Because some of the teachers' values here, they're not values I can support. I just can't tolerate those values getting played out." Martin saw those values that she couldn't tolerate at best as low expectations and a focus on a few students, and at worst as racism.

If left unaddressed, Martin and Hobbs were sure that the core values of many of their faculty would result in poor outcomes for students. The question was what to do about those core values. Devote limited professional development time to conversation? Skip the conversation and find a team of people who shared the principals' beliefs? Try to shift the beliefs through professional development that changed instructional practice? All of these strategies required resources.

Theory of Action

Martin had a theory about how to achieve the purpose and expectations she had for students, and faculty were the essential component of her theory. She wasn't interested in whether her faculty had experience with Weight Watchers. She did want faculty with thorough math and science training, and she wanted faculty to collaborate. Martin's initial theory about how you achieved the vision was that high-quality instruction from faculty deeply knowledgeable in their content areas would lead to students' being prepared to succeed in college and careers. The way you got high-quality instruction was to provide high-quality professional development for teachers. The more resistance she faced from teachers as the year progressed, the more her theory began to shift slightly. She still felt that teachers and high-quality instruction were key, but she wasn't sure she could get high-quality instruction from some of her existing teachers—at least not quickly. Her focus shifted from professional development to hiring.

At Tech High, it took Principal Hobbs until his second year to clearly articulate a purpose and his theory about how to attain it, although he acted on both throughout the first year. His vision was that students would be "empowered to do whatever they wanted to do," which he described as "loving their life, being happy, confident, going to college, etc." His theory about how to fulfill that purpose was "relentless and reliable love," or "knowing students well and stopping at nothing to accomplish what we want to accomplish." He faced many challenges, including that many faculty were not interested in knowing students well, that what he wanted to accomplish was not shared by his faculty, and that the faculty were willing to be stopped by many things, including resistant students and the teachers' union contract. When teachers filed a grievance about the twenty-minute advisory as a violation of the teachers' union contract because it exceeded the 240 contractual minutes they were required to teach, Hobbs was exasperated. "What other job can you say, 'I don't want to work more than four hours?' Teachers are working *four hours a day*. I have high expectations for what teachers should be doing. Teachers have low expectations and say 'this is what we're used to doing.' "

For Hobbs, "relentless, reliable love" meant focusing on students' needs, not the clock. For Hobbs, it meant "doing what we need to do to help a kid be successful—taking care of kids' needs by tutoring, helping them get the medications they need, whatever." His faculty clearly had a different theory of action, connected to their expectations of their role and their experience in that role, which thus far had reinforced their definition of their job as teaching four hours a day.

Need for Change

Fundamentally, at both schools, most of the adults and students didn't see a need for change. Darby Comprehensive High School had a waiting list and was the most popular choice for students in the city among the regular district high schools. It had the highest college acceptance rate and the second-highest scores on the state tests among the regular district high schools. Why change? The rising seniors at DCHS threatened a walkout when the plan to divide the school into small schools became clear. For most of the students and adults at Darby, the school was good enough. Most of the students who attended the school were poor enough to be eligible for free and reduced lunch. One in four students received either special education services or English language services. Most students entered high school at least one or two grade levels behind in English and math. Many students had directly experienced or witnessed violence outside school. And yet 89 percent of students passed the state tests in English and math. One-quarter of students were proficient or advanced on the tests. Average daily attendance was 87 percent, so on any given day 1,140 students of the 1,310 enrolled at the school showed up. And teacher attendance was 96 percent. Teachers liked coming to work and felt respected as professionals. Why change?

The school had been organized to produce a particular vision—that some students would learn some things and that everyone would generally be content—and it produced this vision well. The need for change only arises when there is dissonance between the vision and the reality. At Darby, there was little dissonance until the district introduced it in the form of a structural change—small schools—and a leadership change—Tony Hobbs and Paula Martin as principals. Even then, the dissonance Darby educators felt was between their perception of reality and possibility and the district's (and the embodiment of the district, the principal's) perception of reality and possibility, not between some shared vision and shared reality. The dissonance left them feeling as if change was being done to them for a purpose they weren't too sure about, and in a way over which they had little control. Some of them likened the experience to being the subject of an experiment. The assistant principal of Tech High, who had been an administrator at Darby, said, "Was this change all about the money? I don't understand it. Are we experiments, guinea pigs?" A teacher at Tech High who had taught at Darby for twenty years told students, "We're rats in a laboratory." In order to shift their faculty's expectations, core values, and theory of action, the principals would have to help them see a need for change and develop a sense of hope about that change.

HOPE

Hope as a root of successful and improving schools has two elements: (1) the belief that success (attaining the vision) is possible, and (2) the belief that I'm a necessary part of that success.[2] It is not wishful thinking. It is not "hope" in the sense of "I hope you feel better" (a sentiment you mean when you say it to someone who's sick, but don't think you have anything to do with that person's feeling better). As Principals Hobbs and Martin discovered, even if some people will concede the need for change, there will be little real improvement if change is located outside the main actors in the organization. A year and a half after Tech High opened, Hobbs articulated that the main issue in his schools was that most of his teachers didn't see the need for change. And even if they would admit the school was failing, they would say, "Yes, but it's the best we can do, given the circumstances." Most of the adults and students in the first year of Tech High and Health High had little hope.

The adults and students at Tech High and Health High hadn't yet bought into a different vision of success, a belief that the vision was possible and therefore worth trying for. And they certainly hadn't bought into their own role in that success, or the idea that it's possible for me, and in fact requires action from me. In fact, their lack of hope was perfectly rational. Most of the students had failed multiple classes and had reading, writing, and math skills far below high school–level work. Most of the teachers thought they were working hard and saw that students who did their work learned something, while those who didn't do their work didn't learn much. Teachers at Health High described the most challenging part of their job as "convincing students that academics are a valid pursuit and use of time while they're here."

Hobbs was shocked by how little hope the students had, and how strongly they resisted adults' efforts to convince them that more and better results were possible. He had never run into such resistance when teaching students at a different school in the same district. When he substitute-taught a math class for a teacher on leave, students said to him, "We're Metro public school kids—don't expect a lot from us," and "You really expect us to work?" "It just floors me," said Hobbs. "I'm understanding better why teachers are reacting the way they are, and I'm understanding better what needs to change." On the fourth day that Hobbs was with the class, he felt that some kids were starting to "get it"—"not even that they're getting the math, but they're getting that they could." For Hobbs, this experience showed how much persistence and tenacity a teacher needed to push against students' resistance, and reinforced his belief that different learning outcomes were possible, though difficult to achieve. The biggest challenge he faced was teachers' unwillingness to persist when students didn't/wouldn't get it the first or second or third time.

Still, it was easier to change students' sense of hope than it was to change adults'. The assistant principal at Health High, Jocelyn Norris, drew on her own experience as a teacher to empathize with teachers and to frame hope as a choice: "When you're teaching, after a while, you always have a time when you start to get tired. And it's hard to continue to be optimistic. You see so much. But it's like, what kind of educator are you going to be? You're either going to stay convinced this work can be done, or you're not. People tend to get lost, seeing the same scenario over and over again."

At Tech High and Health High, coaches were supposed to help teachers develop the knowledge and skill needed to realize a different scenario, the new vision. Each school spent about $125,000 on coaches, which by all accounts had little noticeable impact on instruction or learning and was a tremendous waste of resources. However, one small investment in coaching had a big impact at Tech High because it showed that something different was possible, and motivated a teacher to take agency for learning how to do that something different. At Tech High, the writing coach organized an essay contest for seniors. She worked with students to write and revise multiple drafts, and the whole school gathered for the awards ceremony, where the mayor and superintendent gave awards and the winners read their essays. After the assembly, an English teacher said to Principal Hobbs, "I didn't think my kids could write like that, but if her kids can do it, mine can, too. I want to start working with that writing coach." The teacher had had the option of working with the writing coach all year, but opted not to. For the teachers who did work with the coach, it helped for them to see the coach working with their students, but that didn't necessarily mean they embraced the notion that they could or should teach in the same way. The English teacher who approached Hobbs had seen evidence that something different was possible, wanted her students to experience the same success, and thought she needed help to do that. She had hope, which opened the door for her to develop the skills to teach students writing in a different way, and meant that the people, time, and money that would be invested in her developing those skills had a much better chance of paying off in improved instruction and learning.

TRUST

"The teachers are wary of me," said Hobbs. "They think I blame the teachers." For Hobbs, it wasn't blaming the teachers so much as it was having a theory about teachers' role in student outcomes, and thus if he wanted different outcomes, he needed different actions from teachers. For Hobbs, it was a hopeful view of things—teachers could make a difference. To the beleaguered teachers who mostly didn't share Hobbs's hopefulness, Hobbs's approach was not an opportunity but an accusation. The flip side of hope was blame, particularly when there was little trust. There were three dimensions of trust that seemed most important at the two schools:

1. Respect
2. Relationships
3. Integrity

Respect

Hobbs was appalled by how students and adults talked to each other. Things that should have been nonevents turned into full-blown shouting matches, ending with a student in his office and a teacher upset. A typical classroom exchange went something like:

Student: Mister, I'm done. Come look at this [pointing to assignment].

Teacher: I'm working with Colin right now. I'll be back in a second. Why don't you work on the next part, and I'll come and check both.

Student: Mister, come look now.

Teacher: No, you're going to do this, and I'll come back. You need to be patient.

Student: This is such a stupid * * * *ing class.

Teacher [voice raised and irritated]: Jonita, don't use language like that in here. Get started on the next part, and I'll be there soon. I'd be there sooner if you'd do your work and let me talk with Colin.

Student: I can say whatever the * * * * I want.

Teacher: Get out!

Student: I'm out!

Student threw her assignment on the floor and stomped out of the room.

When Hobbs discussed this event with the student, her diagnosis of what she did wrong was that she shouldn't have thrown the paper on the floor. In the course of a lengthy conversation, Hobbs told her that she hadn't respected the teacher's authority, a concept that resonated with the student. "Mister, I really like that phrase—'respect the teacher's authority.' I really like that." Tech High's assistant principal, Florence Knight, was dismayed by students' attitudes: "These kids have no respect. Parents have no respect. Teachers need more support. The system is too kid-friendly."

Teachers at Health High and Tech High saw the lack of respect from students as one of the biggest challenges they faced. It was hard to remember that a student may have lacked social skills like patience or dealing with frustration, or that she simply wanted attention when she was swearing at them, and it was impossible to give all the students the attention they needed. Health High teachers saw the disrespect as connected to students' attitude toward learning, which they described as "abrasive, actively resistant, disrespectful, and rude." The resistance started as resistance to learning, but quickly became about the person dispensing the learning—the teacher.

On top of the disrespect they experienced from students, teachers felt disrespected by administrators. At Darby Comprehensive High School, teachers were accustomed to being left to teach in their classrooms with little attention from administrators, which they equated with "being treated like professionals" who were trusted to be doing the right things in their classrooms. Administrators at Darby had told them as much, and had followed up by almost never going in classrooms or talking with teachers about their instruction. Those administrators thought that if you gave people lots of autonomy, they would respond by doing their jobs well. At both Tech High and Health High, the principals had a different vision of what it meant to be a professional and a different theory of action about how to get excellent instruction, which included scrutiny of teaching practice. For many teachers, scrutiny of their practice meant that administrators didn't trust them and questioned their competence, which to some extent was true. For Principals Hobbs and Martin, however, paying attention to instruction was part of their vision of what made an excellent school, not necessarily an indictment of the quality of teaching of the faculty in general or any teacher in particular. The dissonance between the principals' visions and many of their teachers' visions made for distrust on both sides. This distrust consumed a lot of conversational time, emotional energy, and professional development resources, which were seen as signs of incompetence rather than as opportunities for learning.

Relationships

Relationships are often cited as a pillar of small high schools and a key means by which high schools (and urban schools of all levels) are supposed to improve outcomes for students. Through relationships, students are supposed to feel like at least one adult knows them, cares about them, and wants them to succeed, which in turn is supposed to help academic outcomes. Principal Hobbs and Principal Martin both invested heavily in student relationships, but found that the adult component of relationships needed more attention than they originally realized.

Advisory was a key mechanism for fostering relationships. Both schools invested heavily in it. The principals knew that advisory would be a shift for many teachers, so they spent time developing a curriculum the summer before school opened, and spent professional development time with teachers that focused on advisory. Hobbs believed deeply in advisory, having experienced the relationships that developed over four years between advisors and advisees at his previous small school. He could tell that many teachers were uncomfortable with having a 20-minute period every day in which the point was to talk with students, but he thought that with professional development support, teachers would adjust. It wasn't until the day before school opened, when the faculty was doing an activity that advisors were expected to use with their advisees the next day, that he realized that advisory was not just uncomfortable for many of his faculty—it was downright terrifying. During the activity, he noticed one of his teachers trembling because he was so nervous about advisory. Still, Hobbs pressed on. The activities went on as planned on the first day and advisory happened every day.

Some teachers were naturals, loved advisory, and developed the kinds of relationships intended. Most teachers, however, weren't sure what to do in advisory, didn't even teach many of the students who were in their advisory, and saw advisory as a burden in what already felt like a demanding day of trying to teach content. Hobbs saw and heard the teachers' perspective, but he didn't change course. Teachers responded by invoking the union contract, which said they didn't have to teach more than 240 minutes a day. Advisory counted as "teaching," not administrative time, because it required preparation, and thus violated the contract by exceeding teaching time. Hobbs was exasperated because in his mind advisory didn't need preparation—it was simply talking with students—but he wasn't hearing his teachers. For many of them, talking with students required preparation because they weren't used to doing it and didn't know how. When they weren't heard, they invoked the contract. Hobbs decided not to pursue the battle and made advisory optional. Teachers had to be there with students in the room, but they didn't have to talk with them.

A similar course of events happened at Health High, where Martin changed the name of advisory to "extended homeroom" to comply with the contract. For Martin, it wasn't the advisory that mattered, but the relationships: "These kids, they will walk 100 miles for you if you have a good relationship with them. They'll do anything for you if you have a good relationship. Anything. But you gotta invest in the relationship. It's not enough to just stand up there and think you're a good teacher. For them, you're not really that good a teacher if they don't have a relationship with you. That's just how they work. The quicker people realize that, the easier it is to get these kids to do better academically." Martin acknowledged that relationships weren't everything, but thought that they were key to getting better outcomes from students. She didn't apply the same approach to working with adults.

At Health High, Martin and her administrative team worked hard on relationships with students and made it clear to students that they were there as advocates for students both inside and outside of school. The assistant principal attended a court proceeding to vouch for a student's character. On a daily basis, students came to the administrative team for assistance and were listened to and responded to. To many teachers, it felt like the administrators trusted students more than adults, and "took the side" of students, which resulted in students getting their way, having "no consequences" for unacceptable behavior, and its not being "ugly enough to be out of the classroom." Jocelyn Norris, the assistant principal, recognized that administrators having conversations with students, which resulted in students apologizing to teachers, didn't feel like enough support to teachers: "Teachers appreciated the apology, but they wanted more. They wanted suspensions. They wanted kids thrown out. They wanted blood. And I just wasn't going to give them blood because it wasn't necessary and because half the time, you did your piece, too. I'm not giving you blood when these kids are only half at fault. I never said that to the kids, but it didn't matter anymore. They wanted blood; they didn't get blood, so they're mad. This is our culture." One teacher described the situation as "the animals running the zoo," which captured the general lack of personal regard between teachers and students and between teachers and administrators.

Integrity

Martin started with students when making decisions, which contrasted with the approach of the Darby principal, who had weighted considerations of the adults at least on par with students. Martin described her decisionmaking process about resources as: "I work with what I think is going to be best for kids—the kids that we have. I know a lot of people say that, but I really mean it. I genuinely come from that place. I don't start with what's going to be cheapest or get the most teaching out of my teachers. It's not like I don't go there, but I don't start there." It was crystal clear to Health High teachers that Martin prioritized students' interests, which was not in itself a problem, but when coupled with the general lack of respect they felt from her made it seem as if student interests always came at the expense of teacher interests, and made trust a weak root at Health High. Alice Morrison, the writing coach, observing the ongoing battles between Martin and Health High teachers, noted that there was "not a lot of respect for teachers" from Martin. Several teachers left the school at the end of the year. Some of these were "good riddance," but the coach also wondered about the long-term implications of Martin's "undermining" of her teachers, and operating in spite of her teachers rather than in collaboration with them.

Both principals consistently interacted with students in the ways they wanted the other adults in the building to interact with students: respectfully, patiently, and in a dialogue rather than a lecture. Hobbs extended this approach of doing what you say you want others to do to the adults, too. This was most obvious in his general aversion to weeding out faculty: "I think fundamentally I'm opposed to getting rid of people in the same way I want teachers to feel that way about kids. It's not just one person who's the problem here." Hobbs wanted teachers to assume that all kids could be successful and to work to support their success, and felt that he needed to do the same with his teachers.

Principal Martin was less patient than Hobbs and less convinced that cultivating relationships with adults would get her the school she envisioned. She wanted to establish a "new culture" with her vision, and she was willing to have people not like her rather than lower standards and change her vision. And she was far less convinced than Hobbs that changing beliefs was possible—at least not in the time frame in which she wanted change. For Martin, values were nonnegotiable, and she had neither the time nor the patience to change them. Hobbs also felt dismay at the lack of shared core values in his faculty, but thought that if core values were his decision criteria, he'd have to get rid of three quarters of his faculty—and he wasn't convinced that a new crop of teachers would be much better. For him, changing beliefs was the main part of his job: "If you know how to change people's attitudes, then you can do anything."

By the end of the first year, students were beginning to trust administrators, but trust between students and teachers and between teachers and administrators in both schools was fragile and weak. That trust would need to be strengthened before any real improvement could take place.

IDEAS

Before school started, Hobbs said to his teachers, "You come up with a good idea, and I'll find the money." This was easy for Hobbs to say. He had $100,000 from the Gates Foundation that he could use to respond to teachers' ideas. But he really meant it. He wanted to encourage teachers to generate ideas, both because he thought innovation would help the school and because teachers would probably be more invested in their own idea than they would be in an idea coming from him. He also saw his role as support—figuring out how to get the resources to support good ideas. Nobody came to him with an idea, however. He reiterated his commitment to supporting teachers, and a few came to him with supplies requests, which he quickly met. But nobody came to him with an idea of something to do differently.

At first, Hobbs was surprised. The more he thought about it, though, the more it made sense. He concluded that most of his faculty didn't have a picture in their head of how school could look different, and that his job was to help them get those pictures. He attempted to do this through conversations. He was most successful with helping the faculty get pictures when they *saw* something different or experienced it themselves, rather than talking about it (like the writing competition). But the talk was important, too, in his opinion, because it showed teachers their ideas were valued, and modeled the kind of dialogue he wanted to see throughout the school.

At both schools, the principals were the primary keepers and generators of ideas for new ways of doing things. Both principals were frustrated that most of their teachers didn't seem to have a vision for school as looking anything different from what they had experienced for forty years as a student and teacher. But how could they? Where would the ideas come from? The principals relied as heavily as their teachers on prior experience for their idea of what school should look like. The difference was that the principals had prior experiences outside Darby and traditional large comprehensive high schools. Hobbs drew extensively on his experience as a teacher and administrator at a high-performing small high school, and Martin drew extensively on her experience as an administrator in the city's health system to shape her idea of what students should be able to do when they graduated. She also drew on her experience as a mother of children who had been through the city's school system. Both Martin and Hobbs also had exposure to many different schools, theories, research, and conversations—in short, many ideas—through their principal preparation program.

Their different visions for what schools could look like were precisely why the superintendent hired them to run Tech High and Health High. The superintendent saw a lack of imagination in the district's high schools, and hoped that going small would encourage imagination and result in "small schools doing things everyone says they can't do." He gave the example of a music teacher who taught band, chorus, orchestra—every component of the music program—at a small high school in Nebraska. When she came to MPSD, the high school that hired her only wanted her to teach one thing, even though she wanted to do more. For the superintendent, this showed how stuck the high schools were in their thinking, and he hoped that going small would catalyze ideas and imagination in part out of necessity (e.g., not being able to hire three different music teachers), and in part through the leadership of people who had different ideas.

There was some indication that the process of going small was catalyzing new ideas. The teams of teachers and administrators at DCHS charged with designing the new small high schools generated several ideas for doing things differently. Some of these ideas were decreed by the district, like advisory and block scheduling. Others came from the design teams, like the idea of approaching technology in a new way and threading it through every class at the new Tech High. Many of the ideas that truly came from the design teams didn't get implemented in the new small high schools, in part because the teams weren't sure how to do them. One Tech High design team teacher described the problem as: "None of it was possible because nobody could imagine what the schedule would look like." The teams had a general idea, but not specific recommendations for how to make their ideas work in practice.

Interestingly, the very definition of "resource" is connected to ideas. A dictionary definition of "resource" is: "(n) 1: available source of wealth; a new or reserve supply that can be drawn upon when needed 2: a source of aid or support that may be drawn upon when needed; 'the local library is a valuable resource' 3: the ability to deal resourcefully with unusual problems; 'a man of resource' [syn: resourcefulness, imagination]" (2003). Here, "resource" takes on the conventional definition of supply and support as well as "the ability to deal with unusual problems," which is equated with "imagination." The implication is that "resourcefulness" is not about being full of resources, but about how you deploy them, particularly whether you do so in creative ways that address problems. In the first year at Health High and Tech High, Principals Martin and Hobbs were full of ideas and imagination, which they aimed at the problem of low student achievement. It soon became apparent that they needed to focus their ideas and resourcefulness on some unexpected problems—like students who resisted learning and teachers who resisted teaching differently.

ENERGY

The two principals worked seven days a week, twelve hours a day, with almost no days off for their first year on the job. Both questioned their ability to sustain the pace and survive. In October, Martin said, "Will I make it to the end of this year? It's an impossible job, actually. You either have to lower your standards, or you just will have no other life. I don't see a middle ground right now. I'm literally working around the clock. I see a way not to work this hard, but I see it as a tremendous cost. Things wouldn't get done that I think are important." In December, Martin decided she wasn't going to go into classrooms for a week so that she could attend to the paperwork and preparation for the next day that kept her at school until 8 PM every night. She still had 50–60 e-mails to deal with when she got home. For Hobbs, there were "many days where I was so busy I didn't realize I was busy until the end of the day."

By the end of the first year, both principals were exhausted. Hobbs told a colleague he wasn't sure if he was coming back. He didn't know if he could face another year of struggle. He took a month off in the summer, unable to do any of the things he thought he should do. Martin charged onward, taking a week off in the summer. By the first week of school in the second year, she was shaking her head and saying she wouldn't be back for a third year unless things changed a lot.

The principals weren't the only people exhausted by the end of the year. Their administrators and teachers proclaimed it to be the hardest they had ever worked in their careers. One teacher noted how difficult it was to change the way she worked at this point in her career, and wistfully said, "It would have been nice in the twilight of my career to just be able to do what I want."

The feeling of burnout was not just about long hours. Everything seemed intensified in the small schools. It was as if shrinking the size magnified everything—precisely the effect that small schools were intended to have—but no one seemed prepared for the physical and emotional drain this would cause, and there seemed to be little investment in energy. The principals weren't managing their own energy very well, much less everyone else's, and the schools weren't set up to manage energy very well.

Physical energy, the building block of high performance, was largely ignored. First, school started at 7:30 AM, which worked okay for most of the adults, but was well before most of the adolescents' bodies and brains were truly awake. Most of the students traveled over an hour on various forms of public transportation to get to the school, which meant they started their day before 6 AM. By the time they really woke up, half of the school day had passed them by. Lunch was another missing piece of physical energy. Many of the adults skipped it, waiting until the school day ended at 1:30 rather than trying to gobble down lunch in their 25-minute break, which was usually more like 10 or 15 minutes once they had taken care of miscellaneous student issues. Students focused primarily on socializing in their 25 minutes. Even though most of them qualified for free lunch, they often opted to purchase a bag of chips to fuel themselves for the afternoon. There were also fewer opportunities for movement and breaks in the new small high schools. At Darby, students could go outside during lunch and play football, and they changed classes every 45 minutes. Teachers had two 45-minute periods "off," and there were rooms available for them to use during those periods. At Tech High and Health High, students were not allowed to go outside during lunch or to play football, and they changed classes every 80 minutes, often having sat in their seats for the entire 80-minute period. Teachers now had one 80-minute period "off," and there was no dedicated space available for their use because all the space was being used as classrooms. In short, in the new small high schools, there was much less opportunity for students and teachers to take short breaks and to move around—both necessary for optimal mental energy.

On top of this, emotional and spiritual energy were consistently drained by struggle. Teachers struggled to engage students in learning. Principals struggled to engage teachers in improving instruction. Principal Hobbs wished for a "bulletproof vest" to protect himself from negative attitudes from both students and teachers. When there was evidence that what they were doing made a difference, that was a source of energy. When students saw that if they did their work, they passed the class, they did more work the next quarter. When teachers saw that if they tried group work instead of individual seat work, then students were more focused and successful with the task, they did more group work, and listened to teaching tips from the principal and coaches. When Hobbs saw that the same teacher who described teaching as "leaving information at the dock" for students to pick up or not as they saw fit was now voluntarily checking in with students during lunch, he kept having the same conversation about what was possible instead of abandoning it. But the evidence that what they did mattered mostly didn't outweigh the evidence that what they did didn't matter, and that was a tremendous drain on energy. Students continued to fail courses at alarming rates, teachers continued to teach as they had always taught (even though students failed at alarming rates), and the principals kept doing what they had been doing, even though it didn't seem to be making much of a dent. In the face of evidence that a different approach didn't dramatically make everything better, some students and adults slipped back to their default approach, in large part because there wasn't a focus on recognizing and celebrating the connection between acting differently and experiencing success.

This was understandable in the first year when the focus was primarily on survival and getting through each day relatively smoothly. But it was a lost opportunity to show people evidence that they should be hopeful about their individual and collective capacity for change and improvement and to tap into success as a source of energy and momentum.

CHAPTER THREE

People

"I've decided that the crux of this whole thing is that when you come in with a vision, how much are you willing to accommodate for staff, how much are you going to push? We don't have a lot of time. You either get some things going in Year 1, or you lose opportunities and you lose people's confidence in your school. You inherit a culture and a staff. If you want to have a new culture, it's going to come at the expense of people not liking you. They're going to butt heads with you. I've decided that's a better place to be than to lower my standards."

—Principal Martin, Health High

"Love the adults."

—Principal Hobbs, Tech High

P eople are the most expensive resource in schools, and the resource most directly tied to outcomes for students. Salaries typically account for a majority of a school's budget, with the bulk of that going to teachers. While there is no doubt that external factors impact student performance, there is also no question that what teachers do in the classroom matters, particularly for students who live in poverty. The notion that what we do matters is why most of us became educators in the first place and why we stay. In recent years, the definition of what we are supposed to "do" as educators has changed dramatically. We are now supposed to educate *all* children to meet knowledge and skill standards, mostly measured by students' performance on tests. Historically, as a society, Americans have been content with educating some children to high levels with a high school diploma serving as the principal indicator of mastery of some basic skills. In the era of No Child Left Behind, "some" and "basic" are no longer good enough. We want "all" students to be "proficient," and we expect our schools to make them so.

This expectation puts new demands on the adults in schools, particularly on the teachers, and requires that school leaders address several questions:

- What skills, knowledge, and other attributes do people who work here need to have?
- Which of these do they already have, and which do they need?
- How are we going to get those skills, knowledge, and attributes in the building?

With staff, school leaders are looking for fit, expertise, and contribution. Do you "fit" in terms of our core values and our vision for the school? Do you bring particular expertise? Are you helping or hurting, particularly in the core enterprise of teaching and learning? The mechanisms for getting the right fit, expertise, and contribution are hiring and staffing, professional development, and supervision and evaluation.

Schools have various degrees of flexibility and constraint around these mechanisms. Some school leaders, like the principals of Health High and Tech High, inherit faculties and face contractual limitations on both professional development and firing. Other school leaders can choose their faculties and face few external limits on professional development and firing. Many school leaders fall somewhere in between, with tradition playing a strong role.

This chapter will examine hiring and staffing, professional development, and supervision and evaluation, looking particularly at the choices and dilemmas that school leaders face as they invest in the resource of people. We will see that constraints such as union contracts, state and federal policies, and tradition affect resource use and strategy, but that school leaders can also do much more than a first glance would suggest is possible. The question then becomes what should they do and why, and what are the trade-offs?

HIRING AND STAFFING

Good to Great author Jim Collins writes that "People are not your most important asset. The *right* people are," and thus you need to get "the right people on the bus" (2001, pp. 63–64). Great organizations hire the right people, people who "fit" the organization. A school leader must thus figure out who the right people are and how to get them on the bus, which requires first knowing what you're looking for and then hiring those people.

Unless you are starting a school from scratch, however, many people are already on the bus and you may not have chosen them. What do you do then, and what does it mean to "get the right people on the bus"? This is the central dilemma that the principals of Health High and Tech High faced. They, like many principals new to buildings, inherited their teachers, who had been chosen for a different bus. For one of them, the question quickly became: How do I either get my teachers to do the right thing, or get teachers in here who will? For the other, the question became: What are the right things to do with my teachers? Their responses translated into the quantity and types of resources they invested in people, as seen in professional development and supervision and evaluation, which will be addressed later in this chapter. In this section, we will examine the dual questions of how you get the "right people on the bus" and what the trade-offs are when you are hiring and staffing.

Essential questions:

- What skills, knowledge, and other attributes do people who work here need to have?
- How do you know if prospective employees are the right fit, have the needed expertise, and will make a contribution?
- To what extent are hiring and staffing about my own capacity as a leader?

Knowing who the "right people" are for your school requires knowing what skills and knowledge people need to have, as well as other attributes. School leaders often consider a variety of factors, including:

- Subject-matter expertise
- Curriculum expertise
- Pedagogical expertise
- Age-group experience
- Experience working with students similar to those in your school
- Demographics, such as gender, race/ethnicity, language, age

If this were all that were needed, the hiring process could all be done by a computer. However, school leaders are also usually looking for qualities that may not be obvious on a resume. They are assembling a group of people, not just individuals, and face the reality that few people come with everything the school is looking for. School leaders make a number of decisions, including determining what those other qualities are as well as the importance of some qualities versus others.

At Tech High and Health High, the principals inherited teachers from Darby Comprehensive High School for the first year, but had the opportunity to hire some teachers for the second year because some teachers retired or left the school. In hiring, both principals prioritized what they didn't already have on their faculty, particularly people who shared their vision and values. At Tech High, Principal Hobbs was looking for two main qualities in prospective new staff: a learning attitude and "the same kind of heart," by which he meant a belief in possibilities and a "can-do" attitude (his language for "hope"), as well as respect for students. He looked for these qualities as he hired four new teachers, a secretary, and two administrative staff. He also looked for people who had different ideas about the way school could look, people who had multiple areas of expertise, and people who filled some of the demographic gaps in the faculty as a whole. In his case, that meant looking for staff who were young, nonwhite, male, and spoke Spanish, the native language of many students in the school. With each candidate he interviewed, he weighed all of these characteristics, with learning attitude and "heart" as the nonnegotiables. He then tried to get as many of the other characteristics as he could. With one person, he found all of the characteristics he sought; other people brought some of what he sought, but not all. In those cases, he weighed what was most important to him, whether the person brought something unique and needed to the faculty, and whether what was missing was learnable. "Of course," he said, "I want [teachers] to be qualified and know their content, but a lot of the content and pedagogy, they can learn."

Thus, he hired: a Spanish-speaking woman as special education administrator; two African American men, one with experience in community youth programs and the other with great academic success in high school and college, as administrators to help with attendance, discipline, and family engagement; a white woman as secretary; and a Spanish-speaking Latina woman new to teaching. He also hired a Spanish-speaking white man with experience teaching in a variety of alternative education settings. This teacher didn't have a teaching certification, but had a master's degree in history, had taught English and history, and was excited about working in the school. Hobbs thought he would be a good planning teammate with the other humanities teacher, who was new to teaching. Hobbs thought he was amply qualified and worth the hassle of paperwork needed to hire an uncertified teacher. Hobbs was excited about these new faculty members, noting that they had a "much different kind of energy," and that he felt differently toward the people he had hired rather than inherited: "I own them because I hired them." For Hobbs, "owning them" meant that he felt a different level of investment and responsibility for them and that there was a different level of trust between him and them. He saw it in little ways, like his willingness to ask new faculty to help with something (whereas he was far more reluctant to do that with DCHS veterans), and in the new faculty's willingness to talk with him about their needs and ideas.

Similarly, at Health High, Principal Martin's first priority in hiring was getting people who shared her "vision and values." She weighted content expertise more highly than Hobbs, and shared his goal of hiring people who reflected the racial/ethnic and language diversity of her students, and who brought diversity of many kinds to the faculty. Of the nine teachers she hired for the second year, six were brand new to teaching. Martin acknowledged that they were going to require support in their first year of teaching and that they might not all be brilliant teachers right away, but she was willing to exchange that for getting them to "buy into" her vision and shaping their teaching, which she felt would be easier with new teachers than with veteran teachers. Additionally, with such a concentration of new teachers, Martin planned to provide specific resources to support them, and had access to district resources that wouldn't be available if she only had one or two new teachers. Martin also noted that the new teachers were dually certified in special education and their content area, which would give her some flexibility in staffing.

Martin felt confident in her new teachers in part because she had a thorough hiring process. She did the initial screening, and then parents, teachers, and students on the personnel committee all met to interview and discuss candidates. The committee had a list of questions and a grid to fill out for each candidate. According to Martin, "The most important thing we did was putting kids on the committee. And not the highfliers. When a kid asks a question, if the teacher answers to me, that's a strike against them. Kids can tell who's going to be a good teacher at Health High." In addition to interviews, prospective teachers either taught a demonstration class at Health High or were observed teaching in their current school by either Martin or her assistant principal. This process was very time intensive, but Martin felt it gave both the school and the candidate a lot of information about whether they were a good fit. For Martin, "fit" came from this rich hiring process, which included:

- Multiple school community members, including students
- Clear communication about roles, responsibilities, and expectations
- Evidence of the candidate's teaching (or other relevant work if a nonteaching role)—preferably actual teaching, but at minimum artifacts
- Evidence of the candidate's success with similar students
- Opportunity to see the candidate interact with students (on hiring committee and/or in classroom)
- Opportunities for the candidate to see the school in action

Clear communication about roles, responsibilities, and expectations is a two-way conversation in which both the candidate and the school leader/hiring committee are clear about what they expect the role to include. What does a typical day look like? What is a typical load for a teacher, both in number of students and number of preparations? What specific elements does this role include? Is there a set curriculum and/or pedagogical approach, or is that left up to the teacher? What is the school's discipline policy and philosophy? What are the responsibilities beyond teaching? What kind of support does the school provide for teachers? What are the expectations around collaboration, professional development, and other meetings?

Early in the second year, Martin found that the hiring process supported her work. One of her new administrators complained vehemently about the long hours. At Martin's reminder, the administrator acknowledged that Martin had made it clear what the hours would be in the interview, but that her salary was lower than she expected and didn't seem adequate for the hours. Martin hadn't discussed the salary because that was all decided by district policy. Once she heard the concern, she talked to the district, the administrator moved up one notch on the salary scale based on her experience, and Martin looked for stipend opportunities for the administrator. The hiring process had opened a line of communication that Martin could fall back on and use to get to the heart of a faculty member's dissatisfaction, which she could then address.

Both principals relied on a combination of personal contacts and an open hiring process to find good candidates for the second year. At first, they relied almost exclusively on personal contacts, but soon they realized that it might not be the wisest strategy to listen to what their colleagues told them about potential candidates. Martin felt that colleagues were sometimes "not that honest" about teachers. In one case, a teacher from another MPSD school applied to Health High. Martin considered the principal of the school a personal friend, and called her to ask about the teacher. The principal told her that some people found the teacher "a little odd," but otherwise he was a good teacher. Health High called the teacher in for an interview and found "he was a lot odd." Martin then called a teacher she knew at the school. The teacher said Martin definitely shouldn't hire the applicant, and that the principal wouldn't be letting the teacher go if he were good. "Who do you go talk to?" asked Martin.

Hobbs experienced the disconnect between what colleagues said about teacher candidates and his assessment of them not as an honesty issue, but as a priority and preference issue. He realized that "the people I think are good are not necessarily who other people will think are good," and gave as an example a teacher another MPSD principal didn't want who was now one of Tech High's best teachers. He noted, "I have different tolerances for different things, and I value different things." Hobbs, for example, didn't insist on teachers' being able to articulate standards, but he knew that that was important for some principals.

For both principals, experience was less important than attitude and willingness to learn and be part of the school. Both also sought consistency in vision and values and diversity in background. If candidates were missing something the principals wanted, they asked themselves: Can this be learned? How important is it? Does someone else on the faculty have it? Does what they bring outweigh what they don't bring?

Staffing

Staffing comes both before and after hiring: deciding which positions you need and what is the best role for the people in the building. Deciding which positions you need is an opportunity to create new roles, get rid of old roles, and redistribute your resources more strategically, all in the service of supporting your vision for the school. School leaders make multiple decisions when staffing, including:

- To what extent should I use part-time employees?
- Should I spend all my money on teachers, or should I use some of it to hire administrators and other support? If the latter, how much?
- What is the best role for people already in the building?

Each of these decisions comes with trade-offs. Part-time employees can be less expensive, more specialized, and more flexible than full-time employees, but they are often less a part of the school community, which can lead to inconsistencies and challenges in instruction, curriculum, and discipline. They also put extra demands on school leaders to manage and communicate with more people. Health High used part-time employees to teach an EMT (Emergency Medical Technician) course and an upper-level Spanish course. The EMT teacher was a practicing EMT and the course was the most popular one in the school. The Spanish teacher taught one or two Spanish classes and often stayed to serve as a substitute teacher, which lent a degree of stability to that role. Health High also had five part-time instructional coaches provided by the district and partners, which Principal Martin felt was too difficult to manage and coordinate, even though they each brought particular expertise.

The decision to staff the building with as many teachers as possible versus other support and administrative positions depends in part on context. The decision is affected by the size of the school—the more total employees you have, the easier it is to designate some positions as nonteaching. Most schools have many nonteaching adults in the building—so many that the United States stands out internationally in the number of nonteaching adults in our schools (OECD, 2004). The question is whether and how these nonteaching adults are contributing to student learning.

Health High and Tech High illustrate the issue (see Table 3.1). In the first year, Health High had 32 total staff full-time employees (FTEs), of which 21 were teachers. Similarly, Tech High had 39 staff FTEs, of which 28 were teachers. In other words 1 in 3 staff at Health High and 1 in 4 staff at Tech High were doing something other than the core business of the school—teaching. What were they doing?

Note that these are FTEs, which include part-time positions. Health High had 44 actual people in these positions and Tech High had 48. Some of these positions were required by the district (principal, secretary, guidance counselor, librarian, library aide, nurse, registrar, coaches), and some were required for compliance with federal regulations (special education: evaluation, secretary, and paraprofessionals; ESL administrator). Both schools still had some flexibility, which Health High used to staff a half-time parent coordinator, a discipline/attendance administrator, and a technology coordinator. In Year 2, Health High made the technology coordinator part-time and the parent coordinator full-time because Principal Martin felt the school didn't need the intensive technology support now that the technology was up and running. In Year 2, Tech High changed a teaching position to two discipline/attendance administrator positions because attendance and discipline had been issues in the first year and Principal Hobbs wanted teachers to be able to focus on teaching. Another principal in the same building had no discipline/attendance administrators, choosing instead to "buy as many teachers as possible" because he thought that smaller class sizes would support a positive climate and he thus wouldn't need other administrators. He was also a more experienced administrator than Hobbs and Martin, and felt confident in his ability to manage the building while devoting all possible resources to teaching positions.

Another way to examine staffing is by looking at how many students there are for every teacher and every staff member. At Tech High, there were 13 students for every teacher and 10 students for every staff member. This translated to an average class size of 19. If all of the staff were teaching, the class size would be 12.[1] Even with all the nonteaching adults, administrators in the schools uniformly felt that they were understaffed and that they needed more nonteaching positions. Principal Martin felt she would need fewer nonteaching positions if she had had the option to hire her teachers, but as it was, she felt that the teachers needed a lot of support. She also wished she had more flexibility about how to spend her nonteaching position funds.

In the case of Tech High and Media High, most of the staffing constraints were from district and federal compliance regulations, but school leaders often face the potent constraint of tradition as well. Staff within the building may resist the elimination of a position that they have come to rely on, and parents and community members may also protest. You may need to demonstrate that a targeted reallocation of resources can make a difference before you eliminate a treasured position, whether that is a paraprofessional or the person who does a thousand helpful miscellaneous tasks at the school, none of which is directly related to teaching and learning. Dissension is usually less vigorous when adding positions, but in most schools, adding a position means eliminating a different position, so school leaders must weigh the benefits of the addition versus the costs of the subtraction, and be ready and willing to persuade the school community. And of course, one of the reasons staffing issues are so sensitive is that we're not just talking about "positions"— we're talking about people who are part of the school community.

TABLE 3.1

Health High	Tech High
Teachers: 21	Teachers: 28
Paraprofessionals: 1	Paraprofessionals: 2
Principal: 1	Principal: 1
Assistant Principal: 1	Assistant Principal: 1
Special Education Administrator: 1	Special Education Administrator: 1
Secretary: 1	Secretary: 1
Guidance Counselor: 1	Guidance Counselor: 1
Technology Coordinator: 1	ESL Administrator: .33
Coaches: 1.5	Coaches: 1.6
Discipline/attendance Admin.: 1	Guidance Secretary: .33
Special Education Evaluation: .33	Special Education Evaluator: .33
Special Education Secretary: .20	Special Education Secretary: .30
Parent Coordinator: .5	Librarian: .25
Librarian: .20	Library Aide: .25
Library Aide: .20	Nurse: .25
Nurse: .20	Registrar: .30
Registrar: .20	
Total: 32.33	Total: 39

One strategy that can help both with maximizing the talents of the people already in the building and with reallocating positions is to determine and possibly change existing roles. How you reallocate depends on faculty members' particular talents, on student needs, and on how faculty complement others they'll be working with. At Health High, Principal Martin moved a teacher from advanced physics to ninth-grade physics because ninth graders had not had much success in science during the school's first year, and she wanted them to have a strong science foundation on which to build the rest of their high school science courses. At Tech High, Principal Hobbs teamed special education and regular education teachers by their relative strengths so that each pair had at least one "really strong teacher." Sometimes principals move people around to create teams that have a particular balance—for example, of new and veteran teachers, or of expertise, philosophy, or personality. A trade-off is that while putting people in new positions may be better for students, may play to teachers' strengths, and may create opportunities for learning and teamwork, it is also change, and will require time and perhaps extra support for someone to be successful in the new role. The important point here is that from year to year you usually have some leeway in deciding what the positions will be and who will be in them, which can give you some flexibility even under constraints of union contracts and tradition.

Turnover

Turnover, or faculty and staff leaving and being replaced by new people, creates both opportunities and dilemmas for school leaders. Turnover is not necessarily a bad thing. The question is whether you are using it strategically to help get the "right people on the bus." High turnover (>25%) can create many opportunities for hiring, but can also be destabilizing and expensive, with both the time needed to hire well and any professional development investment you made in teachers who have left, gone. Estimates of the financial cost of attrition vary, but are conservatively estimated at $12,500 ("Teacher Attrition," 2005). This does not include the social and emotional costs to trust of uncertainty and needing to build a community with many new members. Low turnover (<10%) can promote stability and continuity and an ability to go deeper rather than starting anew, but can also be stagnant and limiting, with few new ideas and perspectives. Low turnover often works best when you are trying to perpetuate the culture and ideas you have in the building, and when you are ready to go deeper. High turnover often works best when you want to go in a completely new direction, and your current faculty isn't interested in going with you. Somewhere in between works well when you have a core group of faculty who share a vision.

Health High and Tech High experienced high turnover and medium turnover respectively through a combination of the factors that usually contribute to turnover: retirements, dissatisfaction, and life decisions (e.g., moving to another state for family reasons). For resource considerations, fit and satisfaction, which begin in the hiring process, matter because turnover is costly both financially and for the roots of trust.

PROFESSIONAL DEVELOPMENT

Both Principal Martin and Principal Hobbs believed deeply in professional development, though many of their teachers were lukewarm to the idea. Hobbs felt that the job of a school leader was to "work with the puzzle pieces you have rather than find the right people to fit your puzzle." For him, that meant a focus on professional development rather than hiring and staffing or supervision and evaluation. He focused on "figuring out the right activities" to do with teachers rather than "getting the right people." Martin wanted the right pieces to fit her puzzle now, but professional development was also part of her theory of action about how to get high-quality instruction and good learning outcomes for students. This theory of action, coupled with the fact that she couldn't hire people in the first year, led her to invest heavily in professional development. Martin spent $271,000 on professional development, which was 7 percent of her budget and $12,000 per teacher; Hobbs spent $240,000 on professional development—5 percent of his budget and $8,000 per teacher (see Figure 3.1).

The bulk of the spending was on coaches and time for teachers to meet. The main difference in spending between the two schools was in

FIGURE 3.1
Professional Development Spending, 2005–2006

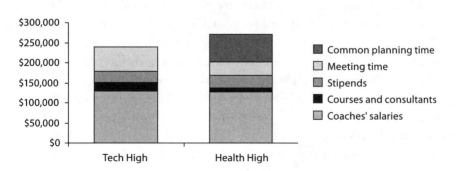

teacher time: Health High teachers met weekly for 80 minutes of common planning time, while Tech High teachers met weekly for 30 minutes with the principal during the second half of the school year. There was about $30,000 of spending on stipends for teachers to meet outside of contractual hours, and some spending on individual teachers taking courses and bringing in consultants to work with groups of teachers.

Although Martin and Hobbs invested heavily in professional development, they ran into five primary challenges that threatened the effectiveness of their professional development investment:

- Vision
- Hope
- Union contract
- Tradition and trust
- Knowing how hard to push

The first challenge was that many teachers didn't think there was a need for professional development. They didn't see a problem with either the student learning or with their own practice. To Martin, the problem was glaring: "It never did work really for a whole set of kids. But there's a myth. I say to them, 'Why do you think it worked? 50 percent of our eleventh graders didn't pass the state test last year. They were all at this school. That's appalling! How could you possibly think this school was working?'" Martin continued to show teachers data of test scores and grades to demonstrate that there was a problem, and then focused her efforts on solving a problem that not everyone acknowledged. Her faculty did not share her vision or acknowledge the need for change.

Even in schools where teachers are more willing to admit there's a problem with some or all students' achievement, getting teachers to believe that what they do can make a difference and that there might be another way to do things that really will make a difference is another challenge, particularly when they're working hard and there's little evidence that it matters for at least some kids. To Martin, it seemed that her teachers thought that the problem—if they were going to concede there was a problem—was the students: "And if you had different kids who were more motivated and smarter and better and had better parents and better upbringings, then the school would work. So, why do they [the teachers] need to do anything different?" Principal Hobbs thought the main challenge he faced was that teachers "haven't seen something, and they just need a picture in their head." He saw his job as helping people to get those pictures, and the first question as "How do I begin to structure opportunities for teachers to talk?" Hobbs believed that opportunities to talk would lead teachers to see new possibilities for outcomes as well as to take responsibility for those outcomes. He thought that talk would cultivate hope.

But there wasn't much time for teachers to talk. The union contract limited the time that teachers could be required to meet: 24 hours after school for the year, and 40 minutes a day during school hours. Both principals saw 24 hours as insufficient to improve teachers' practice, and 40 minutes a day as too short to accomplish much. Both schools stretched the hours by paying teachers stipends to meet during the summer and after school for additional time. Hobbs chose not to use school-day time for content meetings, but did do 30-minute Friday check-ins with all teachers available during each period. Martin organized the schedule so that content-area teachers had the same planning period, and required that they meet for one 80-minute period per week. Some teachers protested that this left them no down time during the day and violated the union contract, so Martin let each content area choose whether to meet once for 80 minutes or twice for 40 minutes.

Both principals failed to use all the time available to them contractually. Hobbs could have required an additional 170 minutes of meeting time per week and Martin could have required an additional 120 minutes of meeting time per week. At Tech High, this would have yielded another 100 hours of professional development time, tripling the time spent on professional development. At Health High, this would have yielded another 72 hours of professional development, doubling the time investment. But neither principal did that. The teachers weren't used to meeting and didn't see a purpose for meeting, and neither principal thought the time would be used well. The pervasive tradition at Darby Comprehensive High School had been that teachers in the school did not meet, and saw their autonomy as a sign of their professionalism.

The veteran Tech High teacher who said that "it would have been nice in the twilight of my career to just be able to do what I want" missed having two periods a day in which "we were free to do what we wanted to do." She thought that Hobbs's thirty-minute meetings might be "good for the principal," but didn't see that they were that helpful for her. Requiring any meeting time at all was a significant challenge to tradition and to the autonomous version of trust that had been part of that tradition. Both Martin and Hobbs tried to shift this tradition by creating time and the expectation that people would meet, but also tried to build trust by taking small steps rather than giant leaps.

The final challenge each principal faced was knowing how hard to push and in what areas—when were small steps the right choice, and when were giant leaps the right choice? And what if something felt like a small step to the principal, but a giant leap to teachers? During the summer before the new small schools opened, neither principal was advocating major change. Said Hobbs, "Part of me feels like if I didn't implement anything new this coming year, we'd be fine. Everyone here has taught before. Everyone here has had students before do well and not do well in their classes. All the kids have been in a school before. If I did nothing, we'd be okay. And, of course, the idea is to do better than that." Similarly, Martin described the first year as "benign—you don't want to freak people out." They quickly realized that their idea of "benign" and "nothing" felt like significant changes to teachers. By October, Martin was more amenable to freaking people out if it that's what it took to reach her vision. She framed the essential leadership challenge as "when you come in with a vision, how much are you willing to accommodate for staff, how much are you going to push?" She decided she would rather "butt heads" with faculty than "lower my standards," and she worried that "you either get some things going in Year 1, or you lose opportunities and people's confidence in your school." Martin was now seeing the first year as a critical opportunity for establishing a vision, particularly when she realized how much resistance there was to her vision.

The principals expressed both uncertainty with knowing how hard to push and frustration with the pace of change, even while acknowledging that change was difficult for teachers. "I don't know how hard I can push people. I can probably push them harder than I want to," said Principal Hobbs. Even while acknowledging that the limitation might be his own willingness to push rather than teachers' capacity to respond to the challenge, Hobbs found teachers' response to change surprising. "I expected advisory to be hard and stressful for people, but it's terrifying as opposed to stressful. How hard do I push? What's reasonable to expect?" Hobbs drew on his experience as a teacher to understand the relationship between challenge and learning: "I think some of it is just like having high expectations for kids—you ask them to struggle, and they struggle, and then they work through it, and it's okay. It may be a little like that." Hobbs believed that learning and change could happen, but not as quickly as he might like, and he was more certain about what it looked like for students than what it looked like for adults. He had pictures in his head for what he was trying to get to, but not for how to get there with a group of adults who didn't share his vision, hope, or ideas, and didn't trust him enough to follow him.

Principal Martin also expressed frustration over the slow pace of change: "My teachers really struggle. They're driving me crazy. I'd go to a charter school if I had to do this all over. And I do not believe in charter schools. I don't think it's really doable. Not quickly. I think it's doable over ten years. I think they'll kill me in ten years." For Martin, the union restrictions on hiring and professional development time created conditions in which change would take "ten years," which she had little patience for since she was trying to help the students in her school *now*. She thought that if she were free of these restrictions in a charter school and could hire people who shared her vision and hope, she could move faster. For Hobbs, the limitations were less about union restrictions than about human capacity to learn and change. Both principals saw the process as a slow "struggle," and questioned their own capacity to accelerate teachers' learning, particularly when they realized that "leading" was going to look more like pushing and pulling.

Coaching

Hobbs and Martin were not the only people in the building struggling to support teachers' professional development. They had coaches. Lots of coaches. Five coaches in each school. Coaches represented about half of Tech High's and Health High's investment in professional development—$129,000 and $127,000, respectively. Was coaching a good investment in the first year?

At its best, coaching meets many of the criteria of high-quality professional development: it is close to the content and takes place in or close to classrooms; it involves collaboration at a minimum between the coach and a teacher, but sometimes between a coach and many teachers together; it is connected to the school's overall improvement plan; it happens regularly; and both the coach and the principal, and sometimes other teacher colleagues, provide some accountability for teachers improving their practice. In reality, coaching holds many challenges, including finding coaches with content and pedagogical expertise who are also good at helping professional adults learn. Being an excellent teacher herself does not necessarily mean a person will be good at helping others become excellent teachers, at least not without some training. Coaching often lacks coherence, collaboration, and accountability, with the most serious gap in the area of accountability. Coaching done well is also very expensive, which means that it's often done with less intensity and frequency, and is thus less effective. Coaches are often supplied and/ or funded by districts, which creates additional challenges, particularly in the areas of coherence and accountability. If the district supplies the coach, is the coach responsible for the district's agenda or the school's? One hopes that these two agendas are aligned, but often they are not. Who chooses the coach? We've already discussed the importance of hiring people who fit the school's needs and vision. Who does the coach report to—the principal or someone in the district?

School leaders face many decisions when selecting coaches—the coaches' role, the leader's role, and effectiveness of coaching.

Selecting coaches

- Is hiring coaches the best use of funds?
- How much money do you put into supporting teachers as opposed to hiring as many teachers as you can?
- Should coaches be internal or external?
- Should coaches be generalists or specialists?

The first question, as with any deployment of resources, is: Is this the best use of funds? The answer will depend on many factors, including the expertise of the coach, teachers' readiness to benefit from coaching, the school leader's capacity to support coaching, and other school requirements. For Principal Hobbs at Tech High, the answer to this question was a resounding "yes," while for Principal Martin at Health High, the answer was a vehement "no." For Hobbs, coaches provided expertise in areas that he didn't have, such as literacy, writing, and "the nitty-gritty of how to get teachers from nothing to doing something," as well as close work with teachers that he didn't have time for. Hobbs also found that two of his coaches were a critical "sounding board" for him, shared his instructional vision of the school, and "spoke the same language." He "couldn't imagine" making it through the first year without them.

For Martin, in contrast, the coaches were people she didn't choose, and who made demands on her time. She wasn't convinced that they were doing better work than she could have done, or that the money wouldn't have been better used in other ways. She described her stance: "I don't know what they're getting paid for. It's not really the help I need. . . . The district is sending out coaches to us even if there's not a match. I asked for some things and none of these [coaches] were the things I asked for." Martin found the district's school improvement coach particularly unhelpful, and wished she had discretion to use the funds being spent on coaches: "I told [the district person] point blank: 'You're paying her for sixty days. I'm sure you're paying her close to $1,000 a day. If you gave me $40,000, I would hire a person full-time to be my assistant and help me write grants and to help me present data. I know what I need. I need someone to do the work I'm not getting to. . . . I don't need a coach right now. I'm not even trying to be arrogant. It's just not what I need. I need someone to help me get the work done because the job is overwhelming." For Martin, coaches were making her job more rather than less overwhelming, while for Hobbs the coaches were making his job somewhat manageable. This contrast had much to do with what the principals perceived as *their* greatest need (not so much their teachers' needs)— assistance with work volume or someone who shared the vision.

A related dilemma is how much money to invest in supporting teachers, as opposed to hiring as many teachers as you can, and how this deliberation changes if you can't choose your teachers. At Health High, Principal Martin believed that since she couldn't choose her teachers, she needed to spend more money on supporting them: "I really struggle with . . . how much do I really push everything into teachers, every extra cent goes into having more teachers, versus what do I need to do to support the teachers? Where's that line?" Martin had seen schools where every penny was in teaching, but those schools handpicked teachers who didn't require a lot of support and had a culture where teachers supported each other, which Martin didn't expect to have for at least a few years. "Theoretically, I think you have to push it all into teaching, but I also see what I have, and I say, 'Well that would just flop.'"

Once you decide to have coaches, will you hire someone internally or bring in someone from outside the school? When school leaders take a teacher from inside the building and make that person a coach, hopefully the person already has relationships with other teachers and is respected by colleagues for her teaching, both of which can take an external coach some time to develop. Alice Morrison, the writing coach at Tech High and Health High, described building trust and relationships as "the hardest thing for any coach to do." None of the coaches at Tech High or Health High had worked previously at Darby Comprehensive High School, so they all had to invest time and energy into building relationships with teachers in the first year. An internal coach has the challenge of taking on a new role with colleagues, which she may require extra support to do well. An external coach brings fresh ideas for ways of doing things, but may take some time to get on board with the school's vision. An external coach provided by the district can also be seen as imposing the district's agenda, rather than focusing on good instructional practice.

A final question when selecting coaches is: specialists or generalists? The trade-off is that specialists can provide deep support in a particular area like math or Limited English Proficiency, but limited resources means that specialists will often work part-time. Generalists, on the other hand, might work outside of their expertise, but there will be fewer coaches in the school, which could help with coherence in vision, communication, and trust since they are in the building more frequently and involved with more teachers. Health High and Tech High both faced the chal-

TABLE 3.2

Health High	Tech High
Literacy Coach (.25)	Literacy Coach (.25)
Math Coach (.5)	Math Coach (.25)
Writing Coach (.4)	Writing Coach (.5)
Humanities Curriculum Coach (.2)	Language (ESL) Coach (.4)
Humanities and General Improvement Coach (.15)	School Improvement Coach (.2)

lenge of multiple part-time specialists. Health High had 1.6 FTEs and Tech High had 1.5 FTEs, each spread over 5 coaches (see Table 3.2).

The principals chose none of these coaches; all of them were supplied by the district, with the exception of the writing coach, who was provided through a partnership with an external organization. According to the writing coach, this distinction was "huge" because she was "the only coach without an agenda." Both principals struggled with fundamental questions of coordination and communication with their coaches.

The coaches' role

- What will the coaching look like?
- How can coaches promote content, collaboration, coherence, and frequency?
- Which teachers will the coaches work with?
- Is coaching voluntary or mandatory for teachers?

Once school leaders have decided to use coaching as a professional development strategy, several other decisions about *how* to use the coaches emerge. Will coaches work with some teachers or all teachers? What are the criteria for deciding whom a coach works with? Willingness, need, content area? As with all decisions, there are trade-offs. Working with volunteers (i.e., letting teachers decide whether they want to participate in coaching) can provide a starting point in a school that's not used to intensive focus on instructional practice, and can mean that limited coaching resources are being deployed where they are more likely to have an effect, but can also mean that teachers most in need of improved instructional practice receive limited attention. Deploying coaching according to need may ameliorate the latter problem and target resources where they are most needed, but can mean that coaching is viewed as a remedial strategy for less effective teachers rather than a means of promoting a culture where improving practice is part of the profession and "the way we do things in our school." Targeting coaching by content area can provide specific, content-based professional development, but can also mean that some teachers are overlooked, most often teachers of science, social studies, and noncore subjects. Again, this unequal distribution of resources communicates vision: our investments speak to what and who we value, including our expectations about who examines and improves instruction—some teachers or all teachers?

Health High and Tech High used a combination of strategies. Teachers at Tech High were getting overwhelmed by working with multiple coaches, so Principal Hobbs asked them to say which coach they preferred to work with and then assigned no more than one coach to each teacher. Both principals had some coaches work with groups—e.g., design a new humanities curriculum or work with all the math teachers—and some coaches work with individuals—e.g., the writing coach worked with teachers one-on-one. The principals also deployed coaches to new teachers for extra support, although this didn't work well at Health High because the new teachers didn't like their assigned coach. Both principals chose to have coaches work with the same teachers all year, rather than focus on some teachers for part of the year and then shift focus to other teachers. This meant that there was continuity and frequency, but that many teachers received no coaching at all, including the science teachers, the foreign language teachers, and the noncore teachers, as well as English teachers who didn't choose to participate in coaching.

Coaches can work with teachers in multiple ways. The question is whether the school has a deliberate strategy of coaching, and how this strategy ties into the school's context and theory of action about how instruction and learning improve. At Health High and Tech High, coaching was determined more by district mandate or individual coaching style than by a particular schoolwide strategy. At Tech High, where the principal believed in coaching, there was no common planning time and limited afterschool professional development time, so coaches worked primarily one-on-one with teachers. This meant that the work could be more tailored to an individual teacher's needs, but also was expensive and did not promote collaboration, a key component of effective professional development. At Health High, where the principal wished she could use the coaching funds in other ways, there was common planning time by content area, but coaches were still deployed primarily on an individual basis, while administrators ran common planning time. The writing coach, at a cost of $36,000, worked with one teacher all year. The literacy coach, at a cost of $30,000, worked with a group of four teachers for eight weeks. According to the coach, teachers felt "too overwhelmed and maxed out" to meet more frequently.

The leader's role

- How do I communicate with the coaches?
- How do I manage multiple coaches?
- Who's communicating what to the teacher?
- How do I provide accountability to the coach and to the teachers with whom they work?
- What's the role of the principal as instructional leader if the coaches are doing most of the instructional work?

With coaching comes the additional challenge of coordination and communication among teachers, coaches, and school leaders. Principal Martin at Health High found that keeping up with her five coaches took a lot of her time, time that she could have otherwise spent in classrooms. Instead, she met with coaches who had been in the classrooms. She wondered if the time would have been better spent being in the classrooms herself. The meetings were important because she heard what coaches were communicating to teachers, and she didn't want to send teachers mixed messages. She wanted to be able to follow up with teachers about whatever the coaches were working on rather than having her own agenda. The flip side of this approach, though, was that she felt very distanced from teachers, and thought that she wasn't doing the work of an instructional leader. Next year, she thought she should have some schoolwide things that everyone knew she would be looking for in classes, while the coaches worked on content-specific issues.

Principal Hobbs valued his meeting time with his coaches, particularly the two coaches who shared his vision, whom he met with weekly. He had less meeting time and less follow-up with the other coaches. In neither building did all the coaches ever talk with each other, in part because they weren't in the building at the same time (nor were they encouraged to be), and in part because the principal didn't convene them. This meant that there was little coherence to the professional development strategy or few shared practices among coaches. The school leaders checked in to see what the coaches were doing, but the meetings were primarily informational. There were no clear expectations or benchmarks—a sense of where the teaching practice should be by a particular time as well as whether or not it had moved there.

Effectiveness
  • Is the coaching working?
  • What are the next steps?

With many resources, particularly those provided from outside the school by the district or a partner, an oft-skipped question is whether the investment is working. In the case of Health High and Tech High, the coaches, at a cost of $127,000 and $129,000 respectively, by all accounts resulted in limited to no improvements in instructional practice, the primary target of the coaching. The writing coach felt she influenced some student learning through her direct work with students in classrooms, but saw limited gains in teaching. While coaching can be an effective strategy, it can also be a waste of time and money if not done well, and can have the added detriment of reinforcing a lack of shared vision, hope, and trust, which in turn makes it harder to cultivate learning.

Why didn't coaching work? The schools weren't organized to support it well, either by having a schedule where teachers could meet or time enough in which to meet. Teachers, lacking a shared vision, hope, or trust, resisted working with coaches and changing their practice based on coaches' suggestions. And everyone was overwhelmed with fundamental non–instructional issues, like discipline, curriculum, and advisory. This all led to a very fragmented approach to professional development, including coaching, because there were multiple legitimate demands on the school leader's and the teachers' time without a clear sense of priority and within a context of change. Within a tumultuous context, teachers understandably held tight to the one thing they had control over—how they taught.

Professional development and hiring and staffing complement one another. Ideally, you can maximize both these levers to get "the right people on the bus" and help them develop the knowledge and skills needed to support all students' learning. If you face limitations in one of the areas, you may need to devote more attention and resources to the other. If you face limitations in both areas, like Health High and Tech High, you will need to pay special attention to using them together in a focused way and choosing strategies that match your context. Health High and Tech High, early in the stages of a significant change process in which the roots of vision, trust, hope, ideas, and energy were not in place, were not ready to make good use of extensive coaching. Those resources might have been better targeted at developing roots, rather than cultivating visible instructional improvements. The writing competition at Tech High, where the writing coach worked with students to develop essays, was a good example of an investment in roots. Seeing the quality of students' writing in another class led a teacher to say to the writing coach, "I haven't been challenging my kids enough." That teacher now had a vision of what was possible, the belief that it really could be done with her students, and that she could do it if she had some help, and she trusted the writing coach to help her. When she told Hobbs she wanted to work with the writing coach next year, the roots were in place for her to improve her instruction and for the investment in coaching to make sense.

SUPERVISION AND EVALUATION

Supervision and evaluation complement professional development and hiring and staffing. A good school leader hires people who are a good fit for the school, puts them in roles that maximize their talents, and supports their learning and growth. A good school leader also gives people ongoing informal and formal feedback about how well they are meeting the school's expectations, and is willing to take action if people are not meeting those expectations after continued support. Getting the right people on the bus also means getting the wrong people off the bus (Collins, 2001). The latter principle is anathema to the way schools have traditionally worked, which means that school leaders face strong resistance, often from their own conscience—"But it's someone's livelihood!" I've heard more than one principal say. "Wrong people" doesn't mean that someone is a bad person, or even a bad teacher (though that is sometimes the case). It means that someone isn't a good fit for a school. At Health High, for example, Principal Martin expected teachers to build relationships with students, which for her meant knowing students personally: "If you're going to be happy working here, it's going to be because you love kids. You're going to see this as more than teaching your class." Teachers who were not interested in doing this were not a good fit for her school. Supervision and evaluation are tools for giving teachers feedback, for keeping the teachers who move the school's work forward, and for not keeping the teachers who don't move the school's work forward.

Effective school leaders wield the tools of supervision and evaluation wisely, which means they use them as part of their human resource strategy, but do not over-rely on them in place of hiring, staffing, and professional development. The principals of Tech High and Health High relied on the tools differently based on their theories of action, with one using it scarcely and the other using it heavily. Alice Morrison, the writing coach, contrasted the principals' approaches: "give people a chance" (Hobbs) and "give someone a chance, and you're taking someone else's chance away" (Martin). Morrison wished there were more of a balance. On the one hand, Martin should see that "supporting your teachers is supporting your kids"; for Morrison, one of the ways to give kids a chance was to help their teachers. On the other hand, Hobbs should recognize that sometimes instruction was so bad it probably wouldn't improve by chance. Tech High had a teacher who spent 55 minutes checking homework in class and was described by the writing coach as "the worst teacher I ever saw." Hobbs did not evaluate the teacher.

In fact, Hobbs did almost no formal evaluations, even those required by contract. This was in part because he was overwhelmed as a new principal, but also because of what he was trying to cultivate in the school. He didn't think any teaching was notably worse than any other teaching in the building, and wasn't convinced that replacing current teachers with new ones would result in anything except distrust and teachers wondering who would be next. "I feel like it's not really solving anything to just get rid of people. The reason I was put here was to really try to change beliefs. At least, that's my interpretation of why I was put here. That's really the work that's worth doing. It's good work, too." Hobbs acknowledged that his approach might not work: "Maybe I'll change my mind. Maybe by the end of this year I'll say 'My God,' and maybe I'll gear up over the summer to evaluate a bunch of people out next year, and it'll be really ugly." By the end of the year, Hobbs hadn't changed his beliefs or his approach.

Hobbs did think that he underused evaluations: "I don't think it's an accident that the evaluations aren't done. Evaluations aren't for getting rid of people. They are a way to move people, and it's a tool I definitely need to use more. . . . I've dug my feet in the ground and I've said to myself, 'I'm going to do it my way, and I'm going to see if it's possible because I don't want to do it a different way.' And it's very different from the approach that some of my colleagues have taken. We'll see if I get proven right, or proven a fool. I figure I can always get a job teaching chemistry." Hobbs acknowledged that he was trying so hard to "move people" in his way, which was creating opportunities for them to talk, having them work with coaches, and nudging them after his frequent informal observations in their classes, that he had neglected the potential positive role that evaluations could play in supporting improvement. Hobbs saw his role as changing teachers' beliefs and thus their practice through "unanxious expectation."

Principal Martin, on the other hand, saw supervision and evaluation as tools for moving people, both in terms of their practice and in terms of moving them out of the building. She conducted all of the evaluations, including some unfavorable ones. She was far less convinced than Hobbs that changing beliefs was possible—at least not in the time frame in which she wanted change. For Martin, values were a nonnegotiable that she had neither the time nor the patience to change.

At Darby Comprehensive High School, evaluations had not been used to "move" people. The only time administrators came into teachers' classrooms was to conduct evaluations, and the high scores on the resulting evaluations reaffirmed teachers' beliefs that they were doing a good job. Tech High assistant principal Florence Knight, formerly an administrator at DCHS, didn't conduct formal evaluations and said she got a sense of teaching at Tech High when she went into classrooms for administrative issues like moving furniture. Health High assistant principal Jocelyn Norris, new to the building, was more active about supervision and evaluation, particularly because in her view, the teachers "all thought they were God's gift to teaching," but their instruction didn't support that belief. She knew that she had to tread carefully because teachers didn't trust administrators coming into their rooms, so she notified teachers in advance when she'd be dropping by their classrooms. They were "ready" for her, changing their teaching for the time she was there. "At first I thought 'oh wow, they're really getting it.' I was always courteous to say I'm going to come in this week. So what they'd do is they'd say, 'She wants to see group work—I'll just throw that together real quick. Let me hurry up and pull out my graphing calculators.' I would literally watch them do a quick switch when I came in." For Norris, the key issue was that teachers didn't believe that they needed to change their practice or that the students in front of them could handle different instruction: "They didn't really believe. . . . They think, 'Look the kids gotta know how to do these procedures; they'll learn how to apply it when they get smarter.' "

School leaders face the limitations of both tradition and union contracts, both of which promote the idea that once teachers are hired, they can remain in a school regardless of their "fit" or effectiveness. Within these constraints, the first three years of teaching are a key, often underutilized, opportunity to select teachers who are both good for the school and good teachers. Before teachers have been granted "tenure" within the union contract, or de facto permanence simply by having a contract renewed multiple times without any indication that there are conditions under which the contract might not be renewed, principals have a few years to signal their expectations clearly and give teachers the opportunity to meet those expectations. Both Principal Martin and Principal Hobbs exercised this option with their teachers with less than three years of experience. They did not renew some contracts, they renewed others, and they resisted the district culture of granting early tenure to good teachers.

Hobbs took as his mantra a recommendation from a successful veteran principal: "Love the adults." For Martin, "the crux of the whole thing" was balancing, accommodating, and pushing staff, while holding to her standards. Both principals had a vision for how they wanted their schools to look and multiple strategies for getting faculty to help make the schools look that way. They were doing everything that research and their own experience would suggest would work, but they weren't getting the results they wanted and expected. They couldn't choose whom to hire, so they poured resources into professional development. Many of those resources were wasted. At Health High, nine teachers left the school at the end of the first year, taking with them the $108,000 ($12,000/teacher) of resources that had been invested in their professional development. Even for the teachers who stayed, there was little indication that the investment was a wise one because faculty were not ready to make good use of it. Neither principal had ever tried to transform an organization with people who didn't necessarily want to be part of the transformation, and they didn't have a clear picture of how to adjust their resource use. "This is really not a new school. I know how to start a new school. I don't know how to start a school like this," said Hobbs. Should they focus on getting the wrong people off the bus and getting the right people on it, and then worry about working with the people on the bus? What kinds of conversations did the faculty need to have to start building a shared vision and trust, and could you do that while you were getting the right people in place? What investments would help people see that students and teachers were capable of more than they believed? How hard could you push when everyone felt "maxed out" and what should you push on?

Tapping into people as the most precious resource in schools requires deliberately using hiring and staffing, professional development, and supervision and evaluation as strategies for getting and keeping the right people in the school and supporting their learning. It's not easy. Within constraints such as tradition, national and state regulations, and union contracts, school leaders make multiple decisions and trade-offs that influence the effectiveness of people. School leaders must also consider their context—are the roots for professional learning in place, or does there first need to be a particular investment in vision, trust, hope, ideas, or energy? Thinking about people as a resource to be managed and used strategically is not about bashing the adults, nor is it casting the adults as a barrier to be overcome, as sometimes happens both inside and outside of schools. People as a resource is about the primary enterprise of schools—learning—and about trying to make schools places of learning for both children and adults.

CHAPTER FOUR

—■—■—■—

Time

"I want to say [to teachers] 'You're working four hours in a row. At what job can you be upset because you're asked to work four hours in a row?' And then you're done. You have a half hour for lunch and you have a 20-minute advisory and you're done. In any other job, it's like 'Yeah, you work four hours in a row, and then you work another four hours in a row.' And then you go home. That's the job."
—Principal Hobbs, Tech High

"I have high expectations for you. Ds and D-minuses are not part of high expectations. . . . This is not a school about just getting done. This is a school about being proficient and having a set of skills when you graduate that let you go to college, that let you choose a meaningful career."
—Principal Martin, Health High

ime is more often discussed as a constraint in schools than as a resource: we don't have enough time to . . . analyze data, meet with teachers, teach art and music, help students who are struggling. . . . It is true that with more time, we might be more able to do all of these things. When there are few external controls on time, such as union contracts or district policies, schools often have longer schools days for both students and teachers (Education Resource Strategies, forthcoming). Even in the most constraint-free contexts, however, time is limited, and there is never as much of it as we would like. The question then becomes: are we maximizing the time we have, and can we use what we have more strategically to help students and teachers succeed?

In a daily context, where time seems to melt away, it is easy to be reactive rather than proactive and only deal with the things that seem most pressing. The problem with that approach is that focusing directly on teaching and learning rarely seems most pressing, and thus slips to the bottom of the pile of good intentions, buried beneath an absent teacher, a sick student, an upset parent, cafeteria duty, district paperwork, etc. And that's a good day without any emergencies.

Though it often does not seem this way in the daily life of schools, time is a resource that we can manage to support instruction and overall school improvement. Even within the constraints of limited time, union contracts, and district policies, there are facets of time that you control and thus can use. This chapter focuses on the questions to consider when thinking about time and its accompanying dilemmas and challenges. The chapter is organized into two key areas: organizing time and providing individual attention.

Time is inextricably linked to the resources of people and money. Time is money, usually money you have spent on people. For example, a day of professional development at Tech High cost $408 per teacher in time alone.[1] That was over $12,000 for the thirty teachers before factoring in administrators' time and any additional costs for professional development, such as a coach or consultant's time. Principal Martin at Health High was well aware of the cost of time. The district high school reform office led a professional development session in the summer before school started. Between the cost of the off-site facility where the session was held and paying teachers stipends for their noncontractual time, the professional development session cost $9,000. Before the session, Martin said, "I hope to God at the end of those days I feel like we have a product that's worth thousands of dollars." She was skeptical that the district-led session would be a good use of time and money.

ORGANIZING TIME

Time in schools is heavily influenced by historical precedent. Most children in the United States attend schools for 180 days a year, for 6–6.5 hours a day. While the scope of what we expect students to know and do has expanded and deepened dramatically over the last fifty years, the time in which we expect them to do so has remained remarkably fixed. More time does not necessarily mean more learning, of course. It matters tremendously what is happening in that time. Examining how a school spends its time tells us a lot about what the school values and about how well it's using its people resource.

No matter how much time you have, the first fundamental consideration in using time as a resource is organizing it, which leads to three questions:

- How much total time is there in the school year?
- What should that time be spent on?
- How can time best be organized to do what we want?

Total Time

The first consideration is how much time there is to work with. Tech High and Health High are typical American schools. The student year was 180 days, 6.33 hours a day, for a total of 1,139 hours.[2] The school day went from 7:20 AM until 1:40 PM. The teacher year was almost identical to the student year: 181 days, 6.67 hours a day, plus 24 professional development hours, for a total of 1,231 hours. The school day for teachers went from 7:10 AM until 1:50 PM.

At Tech High and Health High, the biggest constraints on total time were union contracts and district bus schedules. The union contract stipulated that teachers must arrive at school ten minutes before classes begin and could leave ten minutes after classes end. Additionally, the contract allowed for one day before school began and twenty-four hours of professional development. For teachers, any time beyond this was voluntary and usually had to be compensated. The district bus schedules were also a large constraint for both schools. Both schools would have liked to start later—the 7:20 AM start was well before students' teenage body clocks were ready to learn—but could not due to the district's bus schedules. The schools would also have liked to have had the option to extend the day for some students, but limited bus transportation at the end of the day made that challenging. The final bus problem was that the buses were consistently late. Many students began their transportation journey to school at 6:15 AM, relying on public transportation to get them to a district bus pick-up point a couple miles from the school, a lengthy process that Hobbs described as "a pain in the ass." The real start time for both schools was closer to 7:25 or 7:30, depending on when the buses arrived, which accumulated a time loss equivalent to five days of school.

Another aspect of total time is attendance. The time totals above assume that both students and teachers are present every day, all day. In most schools, this is not the case. Average daily student attendance at Tech High and Health High in 2005–06 was 90 percent and 91 percent, respectively. This was an improvement over the 87 percent daily attendance rate at Darby Comprehensive High School the previous year. Unlike grading systems where 90 percent seems like a fairly good grade, 90 percent attendance means either some kids are missing a lot of school or a lot of kids are missing some school. On any given day, a full 10 percent of students are not present, which makes it exceedingly difficult to help them learn. A Health High student captured the issue succinctly: "You need to come to school every day." At Tech High, that meant 38 students and at Health High 27 students were absent each day. Tardies also cut into learning time for students, and both Tech High and Health High struggled with tardies. Principal Hobbs at Tech High thought that attendance and tardies should be a primary focus for the second year because kids simply missed a lot of school time.

Teacher attendance is an oft-overlooked aspect of total time. At Tech High and Health High, average daily teacher attendance was 93 percent, which meant that 2 of 30 teachers and 1.5 of 22 teachers respectively were absent every day at the schools. As with the students, some of these absences represented long-term absences (e.g., due to medical or family issues), but the absences also represented a culture in which absenteeism was accepted. In contrast to the increase in student attendance, teacher attendance decreased from 96 percent at DCHS the previous year. At Tech High, that translated to one more teacher's being absent every day, in comparison to the comprehensive school rate. At Tech High and Health High, if teachers and students happened to be absent on different days, the average student would miss 3–4 weeks of instruction with their regular classroom teacher. Research supports what common sense tells us, which is that teacher attendance matters for student achievement (Miller, 2006). In other words, if teachers are present and teaching, kids are more likely to learn. Fortunately, this piece of time is easier to influence than extending the contractual school day. There is total time to be gained simply by getting kids and teachers to attend school more.

Common Planning Time

Once you know how much total time you have to work with and you've maximized students' and teachers' attendance, the next questions are what the time should be spent on, and how best to organize the time to do what you want. The schedule embodies the management of time as a resource and is an organizational tool that supports the work of the school. Teaching and learning decisions should drive the schedule, not vice versa.

One major consideration is whether the schedule will include time for teachers to meet. High-quality professional development includes both frequency and collaboration, which means that teachers need time to meet together. Union contracts and tradition are often constraints on how much time teachers will meet after school, which makes it all the more important to use time within school well. Common planning time, or time for intentionally-grouped teachers to meet during the school day, can substantially increase the time available for teachers to meet. At Health High, the contract provided for 24 hours of afterschool professional development time and gave the principal discretion over half of teachers' administration/prep time during the day. Principal Martin used 80 of the 200 weekly minutes available to her for common planning time, which added a total of 48 hours, thereby tripling the amount of time available for professional development at no additional financial cost. This decision had other costs, though, as resource decisions often do. Class sizes at Health High varied widely in order to group teachers by content during their planning period. A chemistry teacher, for example, had one class of 15 students, one of 22 students, and one of 29 students, and there was no way to distribute students more evenly and retain common planning time, in part because the school was small and there was only one chemistry teacher.

As the People chapter noted, teachers were not used to meeting together and when they were compelled to do so, it felt to some like an imposition and to others like a sign of distrust, particularly when they did not share a vision or value for using the time to collaborate. At Health High, teachers in all but one content area decided to enforce their contractual right to meet in 40-minute spurts rather than an 80-minute block. The 40 minutes was too short to accomplish anything, and thus reinforced teachers' thinking that common planning time was not a valuable use of their time and they were better left on their own. By the end of the year, Principal Martin was still committed to common planning time, but acknowledged that it was useful for some teachers and not for others, depending on their readiness to collaborate. Principal Hobbs decided not to do common planning time because it was difficult to schedule, schedule and he did not think teachers were ready for it.

The question of who is going to meet together about what is an important one: meet by content area? grade level? shared students? Meet about professional development, student issues, and/or operational issues? Principals and teachers in both schools saw the need for time to talk about student issues regularly and about school issues occasionally, but with limited teacher meeting time, the principals chose to focus primarily on content-based professional development, with Tech High using Friday meetings for a mixture of student issues and school issues. Health High teachers saw a need for faculty-wide conversations and conversation about topics other than content. As one teacher noted, "The first time we all sat down together was in June. Then we realized that we had all felt the same frustrations all year long and didn't know it. For some things, there were structures that weren't being used. For others, we needed more conversations. How many kids can you write up? We haven't had enough conversation about the culture we're trying to create." For this teacher, the dearth of opportunity to talk had led to a lack of trust between administrators and teachers (with teachers feeling like they weren't being supported with discipline and administrators feeling like teachers weren't using the structures in place for support), a lack of hope from frustration, and a lack of vision about what the school was trying to build.

In a small school, it's hard to have multiple teachers of the same subject (i.e., there is only one chemistry teacher or one third-grade teacher or one sixth-grade math teacher), which makes it hard for teachers to discuss their curriculum and lesson plans with their colleagues. Content-area conversations can be useful for vertical alignment, but may be less useful for improvement of a particular curriculum. Tech High and Health High chose content area as the focus for professional development, but were trying to figure out ways to organize their schedules for Year Two that allowed some time to meet by grade/students as well. Health High worked out a way to get all core teachers off for a block of time on Fridays using a combination of noncore teachers and part-time teachers and volunteers. Principal Martin reasoned that she could then have teachers meet by content or students, depending on need.

Building the Schedule

Once you have made fundamental decisions about what you want time for, you're ready to organize a schedule (see Appendix for a more detailed discussion of considerations about what you want time for). In truth, the process of figuring out what and how is a simultaneous one because both what and how are linked to your vision for how teachers teach and students learn best. On the "how" side, you have a few more decisions to make: How long will classes be? Will they all be the same length? How many classes will there be? Will classes be semesterized? Will the schedule look the same every day, or rotate? With all of these questions, the next question is: Why? What's your rationale for making these decisions? How do these decisions contribute to improved outcomes for students? While it may seem obvious that decisions need to connect to a theory of action about the way they lead to improved outcomes for students, in many schools the schedule looks the way it does for reasons that are either unexplained or simply not linked to student learning.

Longer blocks of time are helpful for students when teachers know how to use the time well. This last caveat is important because if teachers don't know how to use the time well, they'll need extra resources to support them in learning to use the time well—or better to stick to shorter periods of time. Both Health High and Tech High decided to go with 80-minute blocks in their schedule and devoted some professional development time to "teaching in the block." Principals, coaches, teachers, and students all echoed the research and said that the block was great in some classes and not great in others, depending on the teachers' comfort and skill level. One Tech High student described the variation: "Some teachers make class fun, some make it boring. Some have activities based on nothing. I fall asleep." One teacher said that the block seemed like "too much time" at first, but now "it's not enough—I have to tell kids to get out." A coach described a teacher who did not adjust instruction for the longer block as spending "80 minutes doing a 45-minute lesson, including 30 minutes reviewing homework."

One of the main reasons both principals decided to have 80-minute blocks was to allow students time to learn the content. Martin knew that 60-minute blocks would make her schedule more flexible and make it easier for teachers to meet, but didn't think it was best for students: "The only reason I would go to 60-minute blocks is if I really thought kids would be more successful in 60-minute blocks than 80-minute blocks. I think about the tradeoffs. What would I lose? The struggling learners wouldn't have enough time." She cited an example of a humanities teacher who had students reading every day. The teacher "wouldn't have had time to do that in 60-minute block, but in an 80-minute block, she converted all of the students into readers." She concluded: "It's very expensive to run it this way. I'm hoping kids are learning more. I'm doing it with my eyes wide open. Some teachers are wasting 20 minutes, but that's mostly gone or will be gone next year." For Martin, it was more "expensive" to run 80-minute blocks because she got fewer classes out of each teacher. But her theory was that it was worth it because students and teachers would have no excuse for students not to learn the content. Year-long 80-minute blocks meant that students were getting 105 more hours of a subject each year than they had with 45-minute periods at DCHS. That was the equivalent of three-quarters of a school year at DCHS. By the time a student graduated after four years at Health High, he would have accumulated three years more time in English and math than he would have had at Darby. Teachers confirmed Martin's belief that some of this time wasn't being used well. Said one teacher, "I could stand 60 minutes. I feel like I'm wasting students' time." Another teacher agreed that he could accomplish the same amount in 60 minutes, but he saw the value in keeping 80-minute blocks "for a little longer," particularly because "until we figure out how to get kids to do homework, we have to do it in class." Until the habits of academic learning were established, the 80-minute block made sense.

From the students' perspective, the block did make sense. Though 80 minutes felt "too long at first," they were "used to it" by the second year. Students at both schools appreciated the extra time, including the time to do homework. They felt that they learned more and that the day went by faster. They also thought teachers were making better use of the time, with "more stuff planned now," though they felt that teachers should plan more active learning and experiments since many classes were still "boring." One student captured the classroom dynamic as "when the teacher talks, that's when everyone sleeps." The implication was that teachers should talk a little less, and students should do a little more.

A related theory of action that both principals had was that the block would give more time for relationship-building between teachers and students, which in turn would lead to students learning the course content. The block should help cultivate trust. A teacher at Health High experienced the block that way. When he taught at Darby, the 45-minute period "was a joke—a kid could avoid you easily for 45 minutes. With 80, the power shifts to the teacher. Eventually, you're going to do what I ask you to do." Students agreed, saying that teachers paid more attention to them in the block and that it was harder to skip class than it had been at Darby. A longer block demonstrated that learning was possible, a key ingredient of hope. And according to students, they did have stronger relationships with teachers than they had had at the comprehensive high school. Some students said they could "talk to teachers about anything" and the teachers seemed more "laid-back and tolerant" than they had at Darby. Trust between teachers and students was slowly taking root.

Finally, both principals thought the block was worth professional development time because it gave them an opportunity to talk about effective pedagogy in the guise of talking about teaching in the block, which allowed them to communicate their instructional vision while treading carefully on trust. Hobbs hoped that the blocks would make a positive difference and would also help people experience the need for change: "People need to try old things and see that they're not working—or that they are, and we'll keep them. Why would teachers change? . . . You have to see that your methods are bankrupt, and then you have some impetus to change." Hobbs thought that more contact between students and teachers made it harder to hide and avoid things—for both students and teachers.

In the first year, the block did not live up to the principals' expectations, in part because there was limited professional development time devoted to it. There was neither enough investment in helping teachers be successful in the block, which limited students' success, nor enough investment in conversations about what was working and not working, which limited the cultivation of vision, hope, trust, and ideas. The lack of shared vision was evidenced at Tech High when some teachers threatened to grieve the schedule because they taught three blocks in a row. Hobbs was quick to point out that the schedule did not violate the union contract because there was a short homeroom time between second and third block. But mostly he was incredulous—on days where teachers taught three blocks in a row, they were finished teaching by 11:30. Hobbs asked, "At what job can you be upset because you're asked to work four hours in a row?" Clearly, Hobbs and his faculty did not share a vision or trust yet, particularly around what it meant to be a teacher.

In tandem with the decision about how long classes will be is how many classes there will be. Tech High and Health High each had four classes per day as a result of their decision about how long the classes would be. The next decision is whether the schedule will look the same

FIGURE 4.1
Tech High Schedule

		Mon	Tue	Wed	Thu	Fri
7:20-8:40	80 min	A	D	C	B	A
8:43-10:03	80 min	B	A	D	C	B
10:06-10:13	7 min			HOMEROOM		
10:16-11:31	75 min	C	B	A	D	C
11:34-11:59	25 min			LUNCH		
12:02-12:22	20 min			ADVISORY		
12:25-1:40	75 min	D	C	B	A	D

FIGURE 4.2
Health High Schedule

7:20-7:45 AM	Block 1—Advisory
7:48-9:08 AM	Block 2
9:11-10:31 AM	Block 3
10:31-10:56 AM	LUNCH
10:57-12:17 PM	Block 4
12:20-1:40 PM	Block 5
1:45-3:45 PM	EXTENDED DAY FOR ALL NINTH-GRADE STUDENTS

every day. Tech High rotated the schedule so that each day looked different (see Figure 4.1).

When Principal Hobbs substitute-taught one class for a math teacher out on medical leave, he was particularly grateful for the rotation, as he noted that students really functioned differently at different times of day: "The day when I have kids last is a nightmare. First period is more productive and peaceful." Health High, on the other hand, kept the same schedule every day, all year (see Figure 4.2).

A related issue is whether students will take the same courses all year. Hobbs chose to semesterize some courses so that students would take more technology courses. Though students at Health High wished they had more class options, like wood shop, cooking, or another year of gym, their principal did not want to trade course options for time devoted to content. At least for a few years, as teachers and students adjusted to the block and the more rigorous academic expectations of the school, Martin wanted to keep things as simple as possible and to maximize the time teachers had to teach and students had to learn the material. Students took humanities, which combined English and social studies in one course, math, and science. Their fourth block did vary somewhat, and was for foreign language, physical education, and technology. Students took these courses by the semester or on an A–B schedule for the year. Neither principal saw the schedule as fixed and both thought it would change over time as students' and teachers' needs changed.

Building a schedule is both an art and a science, and it helps if you find it fun. If scheduling is not a fun task for you, find someone on the faculty for whom it's a welcome puzzle and tell them what you'd like the schedule to do. There is usually more flexibility in a schedule than might be obvious at first glance. Most of all, consider the schedule a resource that helps you enact your vision.

PROVIDING INDIVIDUAL ATTENTION

One of the core challenges in managing time as a resource is providing individual attention within an overall strategy for all students. Resources are limited, and we can't give everyone individual attention all the time. We thus have to figure out who needs individual attention for what and how to use resources creatively to provide it rather than locking ourselves into a mode in which everyone is doing the same thing all the time. The biggest limitations here are tradition and lack of ideas and imagination, but there are also major constraints of regulations (e.g., who can teach what, including programs like special education and English-language learning) and available resources. There are four major areas to consider in providing individual attention:

- Assessment
- Support and enrichment
- Special needs
- Load

Assessment

Assessment is a key ingredient in providing individual attention because it provides information about who needs what kind of help. In the current era of high-stakes accountability, "assessment" is too-often equated with annual state tests, which can give information about trends over time and about groups of students, but are not as helpful when it comes to figuring out what each student knows, can do, and needs help with. Classroom and schoolwide assessments are better suited for individualized information, as are some standardized tests that cover a smaller domain of knowledge and skills than annual state tests.

School leaders must address several questions about assessment: What do we need to know, and what kind of information do our current assessments provide? How are we keeping track of how students are doing? Who's keeping track? Who's responding to that information? How are we responding to that information? Tech High and Health High underutilized assessment as a tool for improvement, in part because they were so consumed with getting things in place in the first year that they weren't ready either to assess or to respond to the assessments. Both schools used conventional forms of assessment—mostly classroom tests, with some projects and smaller assignments. There were district assessments in the core subjects, but these were not "used" in the sense that neither the principals nor teachers looked at the results to inform their decisionmaking. Tech High did administer a standardized reading assessment to ninth graders in the fall and spring to assess their reading level, but teachers refused to score the assessments and did not do anything with the information.

Health High took a different approach, which was to focus on grades. One of the only unilateral things Principal Martin did when she became principal was to declare a new grading policy—no final grades below a

C–. Anything not worthy of a C– would be an Incomplete. Martin shared the grading policy with teachers, parents, and students before the school year started: "Ds don't help you go to college and don't indicate proficiency," Martin said. "I want to really be about proficiency. It also holds me accountable. If you want to do the work and work hard, and you don't get to a C–, then the problem is ours, not the student's. We have to be able to teach to a C–. We have to be able to teach to mastery. . . . It ups the ante for us as well. It says to everyone that the expectation is that you're going to teach so kids can learn." Everyone seemed on board with the new grading policy—until the end of the first quarter. Teachers said, "What?! We're not giving Fs?! That's ridiculous!" Teachers protested that students had earned the F and that Fs would spur students to do better. "They were telling me Fs are motivators, and I was like 'I don't think so, but let me go look,' " said Martin. She looked up forty of the previous year's report cards in which students had at least one F. "Only one of those students went from an F to a C–. Everyone else either stayed at an F, or went to an F+. It's not a motivator. They were convinced. My good teachers were convinced that Fs are motivators. My bad teachers think you deserve an F if you don't do the work."

Martin showed teachers the data and insisted on enforcing the grading policy. She was surprised by two things. First, almost all students started doing their work to make up their Incompletes: "I have kids who are staying after school and I'm totally shocked and they're trying to do the work. And they flunked everything. I've only had two kids who've said to me, 'I don't really care. I'll take the F.' Everybody else is like, 'Oh yeah, this is a good idea. I'm happy to try to do the work. I'll sign a contract. I'll do the work.' I say to them, 'I don't want you to get Fs.'" When told that they were failing, that the expectation was that they wouldn't fail, and that they had an opportunity to *not* fail, students responded. Their vision of what was possible and their own role in making it happen shifted with the new grading policy. By the second year, students said that one of the things they liked best about the school was "You can't fail. They make sure everyone passes." Most students liked the Incomplete policy, though one student expressed the view that "you should do your work the first time around." Her peers strongly disagreed, saying "We're lucky. Teachers give you chances." One student who had repeated several grades prior to attending Health High agreed, saying, "If this was a normal school, half these kids wouldn't pass, because I didn't." This student had been accepted to college and was planning to go after successfully passing at Health High.

The second thing that surprised Martin was how resistant her teachers were to the Incomplete policy. Eventually, she realized that the policy created a lot more work for teachers, which she hadn't considered. "They hate it. They'd much rather be done at the end of the term, even when I point out that for some things like math and chemistry that might not be useful. Kids might need to get to proficiency." By the end of the year, Martin had reached a compromise with her teachers in which students had a more finite time period in which to turn their Incompletes into a passing grade, or the grade did become an F. For the second year, Martin decided to be more proactive and not wait until the end of the term to enforce the grading policy. The policy now applied to all assignments so that students wouldn't have the cumulative effect of multiple failing grades and wouldn't try to be making up a whole quarter's worth of knowledge and skills.

Both principals continually ran into problems with the limits of time, attitudes toward using assessment as part of teaching and learning, and student and teacher expectations. Most of the assessment in the school was in the form of grades, which led to several questions. What do grades reflect—what students know and are able to do? student motivation? student/teacher expectations? Health High tried to use interim reports to monitor students' status midway through the quarter, but these faded after the first two quarters because reports relied exclusively on administrators' willingness to follow up on them, follow-up that administrators didn't have enough time to do, particularly without teachers helping. The report asked teachers to describe what interventions they had tried, what they were going to try, and what support they needed to help the student be successful. One teacher wrote that the support he needed was for the student to be moved to another teacher. Hope was in limited supply.

Both schools tried to cultivate hope by celebrating success through honor rolls and assemblies. They cast a wide net to capture as many students as possible. The honor rolls had four levels: High Honors (all As), Honors (As and Bs), Honorable Mention (As, Bs, and 1 C), and Moving Forward (As, Bs, and Cs). Hobbs wanted to call the last category "Nearly There," but his leadership team overruled him. Hobbs considered the first-quarter honor roll assembly a success: 100 of the 115 students who were eligible came on stage to accept their honor publicly, and the remaining two-thirds of the student body applauded their peers and generally acted respectfully. "There was no culture of honoring academic achievement here before," noted Hobbs.

Health High similarly celebrated academic achievement. The honor roll posted prominently in the hallway showed that of the 180 students who received As, Bs, and Cs the first quarter, 80 received As and Bs. Health High held an assembly at which they honored students for grades and perfect attendance, and showed a slide show with photos of students taken since the beginning of the year. Martin used discretionary funds to buy two movie passes for students who got As and Bs, as well as rewards for attendance. "That was expensive, but I think it was worth it," said Martin. "Kids were in heaven [at the assembly]. Even kids who didn't get awards came up to me afterwards and said, 'Oh, Miss, we're so proud we go here. Did you see how many kids got awards? We've never been in a school where so many kids are doing well. I only had one Incomplete that kept me off the honor roll.'" Both Hobbs and Martin thought the time and money for the honor roll assemblies was a small investment for a potentially big payoff in terms of cultivating an expectation of academic achievement.

Support and Enrichment

Given that so many students had failed courses and repeated grades before, and that so many of them were continuing to do so, either out of a lack of effort or a lack of knowledge and skill, or some potent combination of the two, support and enrichment were critical to supporting student success. How could the schools use time to give extra support to students who needed it? Both schools put structures in place for academic and social/emotional support, but were unsatisfied with how well these structures worked.

When considering support and enrichment, school leaders face several key decisions, including:

- What kinds of support are we going to provide: academic, social/emotional, or some balance of the two?
- Will the support be for all students or some? If some, how do we decide who gets it, and is it optional or required?
- How do we build a flexible schedule that accommodates different kinds of support for students with different needs?
- Who is going to provide the support? Teachers? Others? What kind of professional development do they need in order to provide effective support?

This section examines how Tech High and Health addressed these questions and the challenges they faced in providing academic, college, and social/emotional support.

Academic

Students at both Tech High and Health High were academically far behind where their age and grade level suggested they should be. Both principals tried to be proactive and set up schools that supported student success rather than assuming failure and remediation. But that left little room in the schedule if students did have problems, which some students were sure to do, especially in the first few years when the roots for success were being established in the schools. Neither school had extra academic support built into the school day. Tech High offered afterschool tutoring, but few students attended. This surprised Hobbs because at his previous small high school, students did stay after school or come on Saturdays through a combination of a school culture in which that was expected and his own efforts as a teacher to entice students to come by providing both pizza and fun science activities.

At both schools, some teachers stayed after school voluntarily to work with students who needed extra support, but teachers didn't want to work with all students. At Tech High, one student described the situation as, "Some teachers have favorites and push those students," while another framed his experience as "Teachers don't help. I don't do well."

Martin described the situation at her school: "I actually have teachers who stay to help kids who they think are deserving of their help, and then they give me a list of kids they don't want to see. If the kids are going to make up the work, they have to make it up with someone else because they don't want to invest any energy in them. It's amazing." Martin had to tread carefully when she responded to this stance of selective hope and energy because teachers didn't have to stay at all according to the contract. As she said, "It's better if they're willing to work with one-third of the kids than with none of them."

Health High required an extended day for ninth graders, but Martin quickly realized that many more students than ninth graders needed extra help. "It's a resource issue," she said. "I'm putting money into extended day for ninth graders, but now I have a problem on the other end that I didn't anticipate." In the fall, Martin learned that over 50 percent of eleventh graders hadn't passed the state exam they had taken as tenth graders at Darby. "That's outrageous!" said Martin. "I don't know what I'm going to do about it." She had raised the money for the ninth-grade extended day through fundraising, but didn't have the resources to provide consistent after school help for other students and/or an organizational design that allowed her to adjust to new information.

On top of that, the extended day for ninth graders suffered from several challenges. First, it was much longer than Martin thought was effective because she had to coordinate with district bus schedules, which meant she had to keep students for 2 hours instead of the 1 to 1.5 hours she would have preferred. This was not only more costly because she had to pay teachers for the extra time (and thus divert funds she could have used to support other students), but also made it harder to convince students to stay. Another challenge was staffing. The extended day relied on teachers who signed up, rather than on teachers chosen by administrators. Although it became clear that the extended day was staffed by some of the least effective teachers in the building, the administrators did not want to fire them because they had no one else to teach the extended day and because they did not want to damage their relationships with those and other teachers. Assistant principal Jocelyn Norris noted that the right time to be choosy would have been at the hiring point. Afterwards, it was too late to do anything about it without incurring serious damage to trust. The final challenge was the content. The time was designed for homework help, but many of the students didn't have homework. Most teachers ignored the Health High policy that said teachers should give 20–30 minutes of homework per night. Teachers said, "Kids don't do homework," to which Martin replied, "Low expectations. Kids don't do homework because you don't give homework." Martin was shocked that teachers wouldn't give homework even when there was a designated, supervised hour for students to do homework, but if teachers didn't believe that students would do it, why go through the hassle of assigning it? The extended day was a good example of an idea that looked good on paper—more time, targeted at a specific population—but in reality, produced little immediate benefit for the $36,000 it cost, as well as the time it cost Martin to raise the additional funds.

Martin drew on district resources to provide specific support for students who hadn't passed the state test required for graduation. For Martin, these students' failure was directly attributable to their high school education: "They don't know anything in math. They could barely solve a straight algebra equation. They've been in the school the last two years. You can't blame middle schools. Something happened here the last two years. I'm not impressed with what went on here last year." Only four of the fifty eligible students showed up for tutoring after school, which made it very difficult to teach them algebra and other fundamentals they had missed along the way. For both principals, 6.33 hours simply was not enough to teach students what they should be learning now and what they should have learned already, especially given how many students needed extra support. Their attempts to stretch the day voluntarily didn't work well.

College

They were more successful in an area with which neither leader had much experience—college. The norm at the large, comprehensive school had been that only some students applied to college and that the guidance counselor decided whom she would help apply. At Tech High and Health High, the principals wanted the norm to be that everyone applied and got into college. Convincing both the students and the guidance counselor of this new norm took a lot of work and energy from the school leaders. When her first attempt to persuade students to apply failed, Martin tried a more compelling appeal:

> We had a site visit from Dell and a whole bunch of Dell partners for two days. I talk to the students. 'What did you notice about the people who came?' And they notice. 'They're all white. They're all men.' And I say, 'That's why I want you to go to college. Until some of you start going to college and taking over some of these businesses I'm going to be begging money from white people who don't see this as a priority issue. This isn't their community. They don't feel invested in it. If people of color owned some of this stuff, we wouldn't be begging for things all the time, guys.' 'Oh Miss, I think you have a point. All right Miss, I'll apply.' They have to see the connection between what's going on in their lives and what's going on everywhere else. That is what they don't see. They have such a narrow perspective on the world. . . . You have to constantly try to show them. This is real. People don't get these positions if they don't go to college. . . . You have to be ambitious. They're like, 'They didn't seem that smart, Miss.' It's not about being smart—if it was about being smart, you'd all be fine.

Martin focused on giving students a vision of what they could do and what it took to get there. When she couldn't persuade them with vision and hope, she drew on her relationships with them and persisted with each student individually: "Look, you don't have to go. It takes five minutes to do these applications. Let's get an application. I'll fill it out with you. I'll check off everything for you. Let's just get an application done. Then, you know, when June comes, you make a decision. You graduate. You decide what you want to do. You at least have the option. What's the harm in that?"

Martin poured time and energy into students' college applications. She wrote a recommendation for every student because she didn't trust the guidance counselor to advocate for students: "I have kids who told me that for the first time since third grade they're on the honor roll. Let's sell these kids because they have a lot of potential and now they're getting it together and demonstrating that they can be successful." She knew the guidance counselor didn't share her vision of students' potential. By the end of the year, all but one student at Health High had applied and been accepted to college, 60 percent at 4-year colleges. The same was true at Tech High, where the Honor Society posted pennants of schools where students had been accepted. As more students were accepted and it became clearer that college was possible, more students were willing to apply. Observing the seniors' success, a tenth-grade student said, "If they can go, I can go, too." Said Martin, "Everyone now is all of a sudden like, 'Oh, this could really happen for me.' It's less for the seniors than for everyone else." For Martin, the investment in seniors' success had an immediate benefit for the seniors, but even more important, gave other students in the school evidence of what was possible for them to achieve.

Advisory

Another decision school leaders face when dealing with support and enrichment is whether to have a formal time in the school day for non-academic issues, or whether to imbed that time in other parts of the school day. If the time is separate, what is the goal, are teachers ready to meet that goal, and what support do they need to be ready to do it? Both schools instituted an advisory period as a way of providing individual attention to students. The idea was that every adult in the building would see 13 or 14 students for about 20 minutes a day and would use that time to check in with students and support them. At Health High, assistant principal Jocelyn Norris spent the summer designing an advisory curriculum, and both schools devoted summer professional development time to advisory before the schools opened. Although both principals believed deeply in advisory, their vision fizzled as the year progressed under heavy pressure from both the teachers' union and tradition. Neither principal abandoned advisory entirely, leaving it in the schedule, but at both schools it became more of a homeroom time for taking attendance and other miscellaneous tasks. A Tech High student described advisory as "a waste of time—you sit and do nothing." Students at Health High agreed, but noted that having advisory as extra padding first thing in the morning helped them get to school before classes started. At Health High, advisory was renamed "extended home-room," which according to Martin meant, "you're welcome to, but you don't have to do advisory." For Health High's assistant principal, the collapse of advisory as "an opportunity to build deep relationships and build a community of learners" was "sinful."

The real constraint wasn't the union contract—the constraint was trust and vision and listening. In August, before school opened, Hobbs and his assistant principal, Florence Knight, were scheduling students and were trying to figure out what to do—they had more advisories than rooms in which they could meet. Knight suggested pairing stronger teachers who took on a lot of responsibilities with weaker teachers so that during advisory the stronger teachers could take a break. A break in advisory would be their reward for other contributions. Hobbs said, "That's not what advisory is for. Yeah, those teachers get a break—after school, or when they're on their P&D period, but during advisory, we need them to be advisors." This conversation showed Hobbs that he and his assistant principal did not share a vision or values about advisory.

Teachers were clearly uncomfortable with advisory and didn't have a vision for it that outweighed their discomfort. The principals thought doing a few activities would help reduce the discomfort, but failed to hear their teachers telling them that wasn't good enough. Said Hobbs, "There's not a lot of love between adults and kids in this school. Many teachers have a banking model of education—they make deposits into kids." Teachers weren't ready for a period devoted to relationship building. Bankers didn't need relationships. Advisory was doomed, even without a union contract. It really did feel like a prep to teachers because none of their previous teaching or learning experiences had prepared them for advisory. Both principals backed off, deciding advisory was not the right place to fight a prolonged battle, at least in the first year. Resources invested in advisory: 20 minutes a day (60 hours, or 9 school days, over the course of the year); professional development time (approximately 10 hours, or $650/teacher); administrator time developing the curriculum and the professional development; and emotional energy by teachers and administrators.

Special Needs

In addition to the many students who needed individualized attention for academic, social, and emotional needs, both schools had significant populations of students formally identified with special needs—students with disabilities who qualified for special education services and students whose first language was not English and qualified for English-language learner services. Both schools also had many students who weren't formally identified but still needed extra help, particularly English-language learners. The primary challenge the schools faced was how best to serve all those students, a challenge that was not unique. Achievement data in almost any district show that the gap between the performance of students in regular education and students with disabilities is greater than the gap between white students and black students.

Students need teachers with both content expertise and specialized expertise to address their needs, whether those are English language needs or special education needs. From a resource perspective, it is most cost efficient to have one person provide both content and specialized expertise, usually within the context of a regular education room. At the secondary level, finding teachers who have both the content expertise and the specialized expertise to serve students with disabilities and English-language learners well is difficult. Additionally, state and federal regulations require that students be served by teachers with certifications in those areas (though they do not necessarily need a content certification as well). In fact, at both Tech High and Health High, almost no teachers had both a special education certificate and a content certificate.

A fundamental dilemma that both Martin and Hobbs faced was that they knew inclusion made sense for efficient resource use and to expose students to more content and more rigorous learning expectations, but they weren't sure it was best for students given teachers' current level of expertise as well as what students were accustomed to. At both schools, the special education teachers hadn't taught content in years—they had taught "study skills"—but now were going to need to teach content. As Hobbs said, "People seem to agree [in meetings that inclusion is a good idea], but nobody's really advocating hard for it. It's what's needed, but we're not ready for it." Both principals started with the question, "What's best for kids?" and then asked, "What are the adults ready to do?" and "What support do the adults need in order to serve students well?" Inclusion would mean a large investment of professional development time as well as time for content and specialized teachers to talk and coordinate, especially if they were working together in a classroom. It also would mean that students who previously had been taking study skills classes would now take content courses, and that students who were used to being in classes of 10 would now be in classes of 20+. In the first year, the schools didn't have the time to devote to professional development or conversation, and the principals weren't convinced that inclusion would be best for kids. They used a mixture of inclusion and pullout classes. Some students responded to their new immersion in regular education by being a "terror" in regular education classes, according to Hobbs. Apparently, neither the teachers nor students were quite ready for inclusion.

The program that seemed to work best was the English-language learning (ELL) program at Tech High, where students' expectations were more the issue than teachers' capacity. Principal Hobbs thought the program worked because the teachers were trained in both content and ELL, and because there were enough students who qualified for the services to construct a special program for them. He also thought it worked because the technology courses and advisory were places where ELL students were integrated into the rest of the Tech High community. Hobbs was concerned that the courses were still "a little bit dumbed down," and he focused on transitioning students out of ELL classes and into mainstream once they had reached a certain level of language proficiency. No students in the ELL program scored Proficient on the state English language arts exam.

For Hobbs, success would be when kids were able to transition. One student was ready to leave ELL courses in the middle of the year, but really struggled in regular education classes. The school gave the student extra support, talked with him, and he finished the year well—and scored Proficient on the state test. Another student was the only ninth grader in ELL3 (after which students move to regular education). He started failing his ELL3 class second semester because he didn't want to be the only student from his class going into regular tenth-grade classes. He preferred failing and repeating. Again, Hobbs and teachers talked with him, Hobbs introduced him to the teachers he'd have in tenth grade, and the student started doing much better. Overall, though, neither princi-pal was satisfied with the way the schools served students' needs, par-ticularly students with disabilities. Martin started to address the issue by hiring several new teachers for the second year who were dually certified in special education and a content area. Hobbs had been in a dual cer-tification program himself, and wasn't convinced that it helped teachers know what to do in classrooms—more that it helped "know what ques-tions to ask." Both principals continued to wrestle with the issue of how to serve kids well and maximize their resources. They were long on com-mitment, but short on ideas.

Load

The depth and quality of our attention depends in part on how many people and things we are responsible for attending to. There are two kinds of "load" to pay particular attention to: (1) student load, or how many subjects/courses students are responsible for and how many teachers they see; and (2) teacher load, or how many students, courses, and content areas teachers are responsible for. In theory, the lighter the load, the more teachers and students will be able to attend to their responsibilities.

With student load the questions are: how many subjects/courses will students pursue at a time, and how many teachers will they see? In ele-mentary school, students learn multiple subjects, usually from the same teacher, particularly in the lower grades. As students go up through the grades, subjects are usually distributed across different teachers. The more subjects and teachers a student has, the less likely the subjects are to be connected and coordinated, which puts a heavier burden on the student to make sense of the material and manage the workload. Sheer volume was what worried Martin the most at Health High. She liked the fact that the 80-minute block provided more time for students to learn content, but she also liked the fact that it meant students had fewer courses to focus on at one time. At Health High, students had three core courses and two noncore courses (rotating during the fourth block) at any given time. Similarly, at Tech High, though two courses changed each semester, students only had three core courses and one noncore course at any given time.[3] If either school had gone to 60-minute periods, students' load would have increased 25 percent. Students at both schools cited the lower load as one of the best features of their new schools. The seven different types of homework and classes to keep track of at the comprehensive high school had been "confusing—too much, too many classes."

Factors that influence teacher load include:

• Number of students a teacher sees each day, week, semester, year
• Student needs
• Number of preparations (different courses)
• Number of content areas
• New curriculum and/or pedagogy

Each of these factors is directly related to time. The more students a teacher sees, the more time it takes to assess, grade papers, follow up with parents, etc. If students have particular needs, such as special education, English-language learning, social/emotional, or very high or very low academic skills, it takes time for a teacher to figure out how to adapt the lesson and differentiate so that those students can learn successfully. Preparing for different courses, such as algebra and geometry, consumes more time than preparing for the same course, and preparing for different content areas often consumes still more time. Finally, if teachers are teaching a new curriculum and/or using new pedagogical techniques, it takes time for them to learn how to teach with the new material and new strategies, and usually requires additional daily preparation.

The question for school leaders is: How can we balance these factors to minimize overall load so that teachers can maximize attention for students? A common trade-off on teacher load at the elementary level is fewer students for more preparations and less content expertise. A typical elementary teacher sees 20–25 students a day, but prepares lessons in a minimum of four content areas (literacy, math, science, and social studies) and often has deep knowledge of only one or two of these content areas. A common trade-off at the secondary level is more students for less varied preparation and more content expertise. A typical secondary teacher sees 100+ students a day and prepares lessons in one or two courses, usually within the same content area, one in which she has expertise.

Health High and Tech High both had much smaller teacher loads. Teachers saw an average of sixty-one students a day,[4] which one teacher described as "a lot easier mentally" than the 125–130 students he had had every day at Darby. With five periods to teach at Darby, he said, "I was haunted by the kids I wasn't getting to. Now, I don't have kids leave class without doing anything." For this teacher, the reduction in load was one of the key improvements—particularly in his mental energy—between his teaching conditions at Darby and at the new small high school. One of the ways Martin and Hobbs kept teacher load low was by focusing the lower loads in particular areas. At Health High, core academic teachers had a load of sixty-one, while noncore teachers had a load of 138. At Tech High, core and noncore teachers had almost identical loads each semester, but only English and math teachers kept the same students all year. Science and social studies teachers, as well as noncore teachers, got a new group of students second semester, effectively doubling their load for the year. One technology teacher noted that the semesterized courses helped with load, but "relationships disappeared—just when you're starting to know the kids, you get a whole new batch." For her, the reduced load helped with trust-building each semester, but she wasn't sure it was better than having more students to know for longer periods of time.

Another way Martin and Hobbs managed teacher load was in what courses they assigned teachers. Even with the limits of small size, only five teachers at Tech High and two teachers at Health High taught more than one subject, and these were all special education, ELL, and noncore teachers, except for one who taught math and science. Many teachers did, however, have multiple preparations. At both schools, about one-third of teachers had two different courses. At Health High, about one-fifth taught three or more different courses, while at Tech High about one-quarter did. Again, special education and ELL teachers were most likely to have multiple courses.

The newness of curriculum and pedagogy is the final factor in teacher load. If teachers are spending all of their time and energy figuring out what to teach tomorrow, they are not going to be able to devote time and energy to figuring out how to help students who didn't learn what they taught today. New teachers are a special case—they are necessarily dealing with a new curriculum and pedagogy because they are novices. That means we should try to lighten all the other aspects of their load because a new curriculum and pedagogy are a heavy burden to deal with, especially when the whole enterprise of teaching is new. Instead, we often do just the opposite in a kind of trial by fire initiation process, so that new teachers get the heaviest load—neediest students and different courses; often, we have them move classrooms, too. In other words, we often give the lightest load to the teachers most able to handle it, and the heaviest load to the teachers least able to handle it. No wonder that 50 percent of new teachers leave the profession in the first five years. We have given them a heavy load to bear. Though Martin and Hobbs didn't modify the load for the few teachers who had less than three years of experience, Hobbs drew the line at classroom assignments. Tech High did not have enough classrooms for each teacher to have their own room, so some teachers needed to move. Hobbs decided it would be veteran teachers. His assistant principal was appalled: "Where I come from, you don't do that—you pay your dues, and you get your room." Hobbs replied, "We don't do it that way. First-year teachers will absolutely get their own room." He knew that he risked damaging his fragile relationship with veteran teachers, but on another dimension of trust—integrity—he was very consistent about prioritizing student learning over what was most comfortable for adults.

Principals Martin and Hobbs viewed time as a resource and organized it intentionally to achieve their vision. Martin called the schedule "my biggest resource," which was not to say that she didn't value people or money—she certainly did. But for her, the schedule was the embodiment of her theory of action about how people and money would lead to high student achievement—long blocks of time, low teacher loads and student loads, individualized attention through advisory and extended day— all of which would lead to relationships between teachers and students and time for teachers to teach and students to learn the content. Even with less than excellent instruction, Martin reasoned, time and attention would help achievement, and in the meantime, she'd start working on improving the quality of instruction through professional development, supervision and evaluation, and hiring. To some extent, she was right. More students were on the honor roll and accepted to college than had ever been true at Darby. But one-quarter to one-third of ninth graders at Health High and Tech High attended summer school for failing courses, and more would have attended if they hadn't exceeded forty absences for the year. Advisory, the primary place for building relationships and individualizing attention, had disintegrated. And most teachers and students at the schools didn't see failing grades or a lack of advisory as a big issue. The schools had the structures for time, but there was still work to do to have the vision, hope, trust, ideas, and energy needed to use the time well.

CHAPTER FIVE

Money

"If someone asked me, 'Can you do what you need to do on this budget?' I'd tell them, 'No.'"
—*Principal Martin*

"I'm not too worried about resources. I'm focused on building a school people want to fund. Then I'll be able to get people to support it."
—*Principal Hobbs*

Finally, we come to the resource that makes people and time possible—money. As a nation, we spend a lot of money on our public schools—about $400 billion (National Center for Education Statistics, 2005).[1] That is about $9,000 per pupil, triple what we spent on each student in 1961 and double what we spent in 1971 (after adjusting for inflation). Much of the difference is driven by programs such as special education, English–language learning, and Title 1, which aim to supplement the regular education program and provide extra support to students with particular needs. We educate more of our children today than we used to, and we aim to educate them to much higher levels. This all takes money, though exactly how much money is unclear. The typical school leader doesn't control how much money she receives in the budget, so we will leave questions of who gets how much to the district, state, and federal policymakers. The typical school leader does, however, get a budget and makes some decisions about how the budget funds are dispensed. In this chapter, we focus on what kinds of decisions school leaders make about money, including budget, external funds and partnerships, and class size.

BUDGET

How much control a principal has over a budget varies widely among schools and districts, but in most schools it's common for the principal to make some decisions about the budget. Many principals haven't been trained in budgeting. If they have, it's a technical training in how to use the software, not a strategic lesson in how to move dollars around and align them both with other resources and the vision to make all of the resources more effective and powerful. School leaders have to figure out what they want to do and what they have to work with in terms of both amount and flexibility. Like most resource decisionmaking, this is not necessarily a sequential process. School leaders often consider multiple factors simultaneously. Four areas to consider when budgeting are:

1. *Alignment*—What are you trying to do, and how will you use your dollars to support that?
2. *Allocation*—How much do you have to work with? What are the areas on which to spend money?
3. *Autonomy*—What do you control? How much flexibility do you have to move money and budget items around?
4. *Adequacy*—Do you have enough money to do what you want to do? If not, is it essential or wishful? If essential, where will you get more money?

Alignment—What are you trying to do, and how will you use your dollars to support that?

How you spend your dollars shows what you value. A budget is a synthesis of the resources of time, people, and money. You have to figure out who you want doing what and what the implications of the schedule are (e.g., do you need part-time people?). You also have to decide what your priorities are, since most schools have a finite pot of money and can't do everything they might like to do. As we saw in Chapter 3's discussion of scheduling, the key is that the budget isn't driving decisionmaking; other decisions are driving the budget. In other words, you start with the question, "What are we trying to do here?" rather than the question, "What does the budget allow us to do?" This is not to say that you're dreaming with no basis in reality—but first, you have to articulate your vision for what you'd like to do, and then figure out how to align your resources to support that vision. Otherwise, you run the risk of being limited by what's already in place, which is often a product of years of decisions or nondecisions that don't necessarily support your vision.

At Health High, Principal Martin's vision was that every student would demonstrate proficiency in a rigorous curriculum and be prepared to succeed in college and in the work force. To reach this vision, she thought the school needed high-quality teaching, extra time and support for students, respect for students, and family involvement. Thus, she wanted her budget to support several things that hadn't been in the school before— extensive professional development for teachers, an extended school day, a laptop for every student, and a parent coordinator.

At Tech High, Principal Hobbs also wanted a school where every student would demonstrate proficiency and be prepared to succeed after high school. He wanted a school of engaged students and teachers, built on respect, relationships, and individual attention. He thought the school needed high-quality teaching, time for teachers and students to build relationships, and engagement through the school's theme of technology. Thus, he wanted the budget to support extensive professional development for teachers, time for conversations among faculty, students, and the school community, and a range of technology. Hobbs chose to create multimedia computer labs and a portable classroom set of laptops rather than laptops for every student because laptops were expensive to lease and maintain, required infrastructure he didn't have, and couldn't run some of the high-powered multimedia programs that he could make available in the lab. He also wasn't sure teachers would use the laptops well in classrooms. Both principals aligned expenditures to their vision, with their decisions based on their theories of action about how to attain that vision.

For both schools, the theme of the school played a role in the principals' decisionmaking about the budget. Both schools faced the challenge that the amount of money they received was not affected by the school's theme, and both schools had expensive themes—or at least chose to implement them in expensive ways. "It's very easy to see how a theme-based school becomes theme-based in name only," observed Martin. "I'm not given one extra penny to buy technology stuff. I'm not given one extra penny to buy health materials." She wanted to offer an EMT course at the school. An outside partner was willing to provide an instructor for the course at no charge, but the supplies for the course cost $15,000 (books, software, dummies, etc.). "It's the only health course I've got," said Martin, as she tried to make it work. Before the school opened, she had thirty–four computers, or about one for every nine students, and one science lab. She thought this was inadequate to support a health theme that reflected the science and technology skills students needed to be successful in health careers. Similarly, Hobbs saw the cost of running a technology school as high because of the equipment, software, and upkeep needed. Hobbs noted that there were few technology schools in the country and thought that the reason was the cost. For school leaders, the question is, does a theme help define and promote a particular vision, hope, trust, ideas, or energy? Could you reap the benefits of a theme with a less expensive theme?

Allocation—How much money do you have to work with? What are the areas on which to spend money?

Once you have ideas about how you'd like to use your money, the next questions are about allocation. How much money you have to work with depends on how many total dollars are allocated and what percentage of those dollars are reported on the school-level budget. The amount of money reported on schools budgets varies. At one end of the continuum are charter schools, which receive all of their dollars directly. At the other end of the continuum are some district schools, in which

FIGURE 5.1

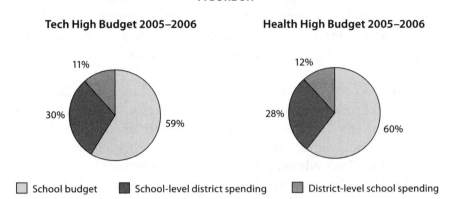

Tech High Budget 2005–2006

11%

30%

59%

Health High Budget 2005–2006

12%

28%

60%

☐ School budget   ■ School-level district spending   ■ District-level school spending

all expenditures are controlled in the district central office. Most schools fall somewhere in between, with some money reported on the school budget and other money reported on the district budget. Of the money reported on the district budget, some is allocated to people and services that apply directly to a particular school, such as utilities for the school building or an instructional coach, and some is allocated to district-level services that are for all schools, such as the superintendent and other central office personnel and transportation. A complete representation of a school's budget includes all of these categories.

Tech High's total operating budget in the first year was $5.3 million, of which 59 percent was on the school budget, 30 percent was on the district budget but seen at the school, and 11 percent was the school's share of district-level expenses (see Figure 5.1). Health High's total operating budget was $4.3 million, of which 60 percent was on the school budget, 28 percent was on the district budget but seen at the school, and 12 percent was the school's share of district-level expenses.[2] About 60 percent of the total expenditures appeared on the school's budget, with an additional 30 percent spent directly on the schools at the district level.

This translated to about $14,000 per pupil at the schools. When adjusted for student need, the per-pupil expenditure was about $10,000 (see Appendix 1 for exact figures).[3] The dollars were spent on instruction (teachers, books), operations (maintenance, utilities), pupil services (guidance, attendance), instructional support (professional development, technology assistance, librarian), administration (principal and other administrators), and business services. At Tech High and Health High, the dollars were allocated across these categories, as shown in Figure 5.2.

Instruction and instructional support accounted for approximately 60 percent of the schools' budgets, with pupil services an additional approximate 15 percent. The schools' budgets were very similar at the level of broad categories, with slight variations driven by their difference in size (e.g., Health High's administrative costs per pupil were higher because the school had the same number of administrators as Tech High, but fewer students) and emphases (e.g., Health High provided more pupil services and professional development than Tech High, while Tech High focused more dollars on instruction).

Autonomy—What do you control? How much flexibility do you have to move money around?

Though Tech High's budget was $5.3 million, Hobbs only controlled about one-third of that total. School leaders must be creative with whatever part of the budget they control, shifting, combining, and deleting dollars and positions to implement their vision. The continuum of control ranges from "none" to "positional" to "total." Some schools control none of their budget. That is less common today than it was ten or twenty years ago, but there are still schools that control none of their budget, or perhaps only a small "supplies" line item. Some schools, like charter schools, control all of their budget, including decisions about how much to pay employees. In between fall the majority of schools, which range from little control to "positional" control, in which schools follow union salary schedules, but have discretion over which positions to staff and other budget decisions. The span of control is determined by federal, state, and district policies, as well as union contracts, which may be everything from teacher contracts to custodial contracts.

Tech High and Health High fell in the middle to lower-middle range of the continuum. Tech High controlled 36 percent of its budget and Health High controlled 48 percent of its budget, with the difference caused by

FIGURE 5.2
Per Pupil Spending by Category
Tech High and Health High, 2005–2006

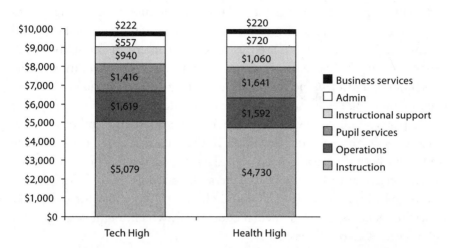

Tech High's having more English-language learners and thus more externally-required positions. In these schools, "control" meant that the school had some choice about how to spend money. By federal and state regulations, the schools had to have special education and English-language learner teachers and administrators, who by district policy were allotted based on the number of students who qualified for those services. Similarly, by district mandate, each school had to have a guidance counselor, a part-time librarian and librarian aide, a part–time nurse, a principal, and an assistant principal. The remaining funds were under the school's control, which in this case meant that the principals decided which positions to staff and what to do with the remaining funds.

For both principals, it felt like there was little wiggle room in the budget. After staffing with enough teachers to teach courses, each school had under $200,000 left in the budget the district had given them. Martin had hoped to pay for someone to help with attendance, discipline, and family engagement, but decided that was a "luxury" she couldn't afford; instead, she paid for part-time teachers, the EMT class, and books and supplies with her remaining dollars. She had also hoped to have some money to pay students for a peer leadership program and for doing things like working on the student handbook, but she didn't have funds for those things either.

In any organization's budget, a large percentage of the budget goes to personnel salaries, and schools are no different. At Tech High and Health High, salaries accounted for over 90 percent of the school budget.[4] In many schools, leaders have little or no discretion over most of the personnel's salaries, which are determined by union agreements. However, in some places, school leaders can decide whether to hire more or less expensive employees, which generally aligns with number of years of experience and level of education. In these cases, school leaders make trade-offs between less experienced, less expensive teachers and more experienced, more expensive teachers. In schools with more discretion over hiring, school leaders could choose to pay more for particular expertise (such as math or special education), which might or might not align with years of experience.

Even when school leaders don't control salaries, they often have some discretion over which positions are staffed. For Hobbs, this decision-making power was a challenge at budgeting time. He was supposed to design his budget with his School Council, a governance group of administrators, teachers, and parents. There were two problems with this: (1) He didn't have a School Council in place by December, when budget decisions for the next school year were supposed to be happening, and (2) In Hobbs's words, "It's jobs." He wasn't sure whom to consult about the budget and was reluctant to talk with teachers because there were job implications for his decisions. Hobbs felt he didn't have a lot of flexibility in his budget, but the move to humanities for Year 2 meant that there would be an excess of social studies and English teachers, so Hobbs was trying to structure things to "lose the person he wanted to lose" and to change a literacy position to a math position. Hobbs experimented with a few possibilities in the budget, but ended up making few changes due to a combination of readiness and uncertainty. He wanted to move toward full inclusion with special education and ELL students, which might affect staffing, but felt that the staff "wasn't ready for it." He didn't want to make radical changes to staffing because of uncertainty around courses and curriculum—he didn't want to eliminate a position and then find out later that he needed it. On top of that, Hobbs was committed to cultivating trust, which for him meant, "My main goal is not to get rid of anybody." A final part of the challenge was that the budgeting for the next school year happened in December, when Hobbs was still figuring out how well his current staffing and budgeting were working.

Adequacy—Do you have enough money to do what you want to do? If not, is it essential or wishful? If essential, where will you get more money?

"I don't have enough money. It's my biggest worry," said Martin several months before she started her first school year at Health High. She wanted to give every student a laptop, which would cost about $100,000 a year, and she wanted to offer a two-hour extended day program for ninth graders, which would cost at least $50,000. At first glance, neither of these was possible within her budget. Then, she quietly moved people around. The school was offering humanities, and had two social studies, four English, and two special education English teachers. She didn't need all of those people for humanities, but had to put the people somewhere. One of the social studies teachers wanted to teach special education math courses, so Martin moved him and eliminated a social studies position, which freed up $65,000, which she put into a "contracts" line item over which she had discretion. By June, Martin had raised some additional money, but was still short about $25,000. She decided to sign a contract for the laptops: "I don't have the money yet, but I will. It'll just work. It has to work." One of the administrators she hired moved out of a teaching position Martin didn't need, so she converted that position into cash. Martin said, "You do have to be incredibly creative with the budget. That is the one skill I would say, thank God I walked in knowing budgets. Everyone else is saying my money's tied up in personnel, and I'm saying, it doesn't have to be that way."

These moves generated enough funds for laptops, but at the start of the school year, Martin still needed $25,000 to pay for the first hour of the extended day program. She ran the extended day program anyway, with one hour of homework help and one hour of activities provided by a local community center. Because there was no money to pay teachers, administrators ran the homework help. Martin thought that if they didn't start the year with it, it would be impossible to get students to stay longer once she had funds. And she thought the extended day was crucial: "I have to have these programs. These kids aren't going to make it if I don't have these programs." Martin spent much of the summer and fall raising money to fund the extended day program and other things she deemed essential. By midfall, she had enough dollars to pay teachers to offer homework help, but she wished she had more dollars to provide extra help for more students.

While Martin focused on supplementing a budget she felt was inadequate, Hobbs had a less clear vision of what he would spend extra money on and focused instead on "building a school that people would want to fund." Based on his previous experience at a small school that raised large amounts of money to support its programming, Hobbs was confident that he would be able to get resources to support the school once the school demonstrated that it would use the funds well and had specific needs that funders could help address. Hobbs wanted his faculty to help decide how to spend money, in contrast to Martin, who had distinct ideas about how she wanted to spend the money and sought little input from her faculty. Hobbs wanted to create a culture of "you come up with a good idea and I'll find the money," though ideas were slow in coming.

Martin's and Hobbs's approach to budgeting reflected their visions—for Hobbs, work with what you have; for Martin, work on having what you want—and their experience—for Hobbs, little experience with budgeting and evidence that "if you build it, resources will come"; for Martin, much experience with budgeting and no patience for waiting for the resources to come to her. Alignment, allocation, autonomy, and adequacy were issues they considered with all of their resources, but were particularly relevant for thinking about how to spend their dollars.

EXTERNAL FUNDS AND PARTNERSHIPS

"Thank God we have the Gates money. I don't know what we'd do without the Gates money," said Martin two months before the school year started. Each school received $300/student from the Bill & Melinda

Gates Foundation, which meant $90,000 for Health High. The money was intended to help with start-up costs, and the schools would receive $300/student each of their first three years. Hobbs described Tech High's $100,000 in Gates Foundation support as a "big, nice cushion." For both school leaders, external dollars and partnerships played a significant role and helped with all four budget "As": they increased allocation, autonomy, and adequacy, and helped with alignment—all of which helped them do what they were trying to do. Decisions and considerations about external funds and partnerships include:

1. *Purpose*—Do we need external funds and partnerships? If so, for what? How do I align external funds and partnerships with the vision? What are the priorities?
2. *Flexibility*—How much discretion do I have over the resources provided by the external funder?
3. *Management*—What kind of investment of time and money is required to manage the external dollars and partnerships? Is it worth the investment? How am I going to keep track of what I spend money on and whether it's a wise investment?

Purpose—Do we need external funds and partnerships? If so, for what? How do I align external funds and partnerships with the vision? What are the priorities?

Connected to the question of adequacy is considering whether the school needs external funds and partnerships and if so, for what purpose and how that connects to the vision. In addition to the Gates Foundation money, Martin raised $100,000 for the extended day program, scholarships, awards, and miscellaneous student expenses. She thought she needed to raise $200,000/year, or about $660/student, to provide everything that was essential for students and teachers. Hobbs felt the Gates Foundation money sufficed for the first year, and in fact didn't use all of it, leaving $11,000 to use in Year 2. For both principals, an early decision was what to spend the Gates money on and how to prioritize what needed to happen first. Hobbs worried about his ability to make decisions about spending money on his own, and started a leadership team immediately to help him think about how to spend the money. Both principals prioritized professional development for teachers as a major area of spending, using the Gates money primarily to extend the time available for professional development, as well as to provide external expertise such as coaches and consultants.

In addition, both Martin and Hobbs established multiple partnerships directly tied to what they wanted to do and turned down partnerships that didn't fit their most important needs. Health High's partnerships included City Write[5], a program focused on student writing; College Bound, local university students who worked with seniors on college applications; and health organizations, which provided internships for students and the EMT instructor. Tech High's partnerships included City Write; Teen Power, a program focused on giving teens voice; and media outlets, which provided technology and volunteer technical assistance. Most of the partnerships provided people with particular expertise, and most of the people came at some, but low, cost to the school: City Write paid for half a writing coach's time[6]; College Bound's university students volunteered at no cost, and Martin paid for the volunteer coordinator's time; the EMT instructor was paid by her host health organization, and Martin paid for course materials; Teen Power and Hobbs shared the cost of personnel. Both principals actively sought out partnerships, particularly those that supported their theme and that provided help and expertise for something they valued, but couldn't do, like weekly help for seniors with college applications or working with the faculty on advisory and teen voice. The principals' visions and priorities differed, and thus their partnerships differed: college and rigorous health courses and opportunities were a priority for Martin; for Hobbs, advisory, writing, and technology experiences were a priority, leading him to pay for more of the writing coach's time than Martin, build a multimedia computer lab, and leave his college support to his guidance counselor.

Flexibility—How much control do I have over the resources provided by the external funder?

External partners were critical for the new small schools in providing both flexibility and services that the school otherwise wouldn't be able to provide and in helping to ease and address constraints. According to the terms of the Gates Foundation grant, the schools couldn't use the money for faculty positions, but otherwise had wide discretion over how they spent the funds. Both principals saw this flexibility as key.

While it was easier to establish partnerships and raise money for particular purposes (e.g., Health High's extended day program), both principals appreciated having some funds that weren't earmarked for any particular purpose. Martin kept a separate school checking account for general donations, which she called her "slush fund" and used for things like renting buses for field trips, ski trips, movie tickets, and other incentives for kids. All of the money was reported and accounted for, but she didn't have to file paperwork requests to use it, and thus could do things with the money quickly. When Hobbs received a check for $1,000, he responded with enthusiasm, "This is great. We can buy lots of stuff with this. And it's great to have money I don't have to do requisitions for." The $1,000 did not bring with it the cost of Hobbs's time to complete paperwork.

Management—What kind of investment of time and money is required to manage the external dollars and partnerships? Is it worth the investment? How am I going to keep track of what I spend money on and whether it's a wise investment?

While the $1,000 was cost free, managing the paperwork and the people connected with external funders and partnerships usually requires an investment of time and money. Both Martin and Hobbs considered this investment when deciding whether to accept dollars and partnerships and whether to continue existing partnerships. For Martin, the College Bound program and the City Write coach cost about the same amount of money—$8,000—but the College Bound program felt like a much better investment to her. For that money, she got over a dozen volunteers to work with seniors weekly, she had few management responsibilities since the program was coordinated by a highly competent person, and the benefits were clear as seniors were admitted to college. The City Write coach, on the other hand, ended up working with only one teacher because Martin didn't have time to figure out how to use the coach better, and she saw little evidence that teacher practice or student learning changed. For her second year, Martin doubled her investment in College Bound so that she could expand the program to work with her juniors and didn't repartner with City Write. Hobbs, on the other hand, saw the benefit of the City Write coach (Alice Morrison, the same person who worked with Health High) in the writing contest, and doubled his investment in the coach for the second year so that she could work with more teachers.

Both principals weighed the time it would take to get the funds or establish and manage a partnership against the possible payoff, both in terms of magnitude and alignment with their goals and vision. If the ratio of time to payoff was large, as with small grants or management-intensive partnerships, the principals didn't pursue them because their time was too scarce. If the ratio of time to payoff was small, the principals pursued them, even if there was some uncertainty. Martin applied for a $40,000 grant sponsored by city businesses, which consumed many hours of her time in preparing the application and a full day presenting to the business leaders, but she had heard that finalists usually received most of what they requested. If she got the money, she could expand her extended day program to include tenth graders. Thus, her time potentially translated into increased class time for her students, and it was worth it to her.

Though she appreciated the external resources, Martin saw them as "lots of things to manage." She wished she could pay someone to write grants and oversee the partnerships, but she didn't want to allot resources to that position at the expense of providing a service to her students. Instead, the management time and energy came entirely from Martin, which pulled her attention away from everyday issues at school and contributed to her burnout. Martin also found it difficult to manage her approximately $200,000 in external funds because the money was in several different places and she had no central database to keep track of everything and what it was spent on.

External funds and partnerships provided critical support in the area of hope—helping students and teachers see not only that something different was possible, but was possible for them and because of them. At Health

High, 97 percent of seniors applied and were accepted to college. Investments: College Bound volunteers, $8,000 for College Bound coordinator, application fees if not waived based on need, and Martin's time in supporting students to complete applications. At Tech High, an essay contest rewarded students' performance and prompted a teacher to request time with the writing coach so that her kids would write "like that." Investments: one quarter of writing coach's time (half funded by City Write; $2,500 paid by school), $300 in prizes for students, one hour for school-wide assembly, time from the mayor and superintendent, and English class time devoted to writing and revising, part of the curriculum.

A final example was a robotics competition that Martin described as "defining" for Health High. Martin and teachers recruited several students to build a robot after school. Neither the students nor the two teachers who worked with them had ever built a robot. They entered their robot in a competition with forty-three other schools from all over the country. Their robot was, by Martin's description, the "homeliest looking robot," in part because Health High could only afford one of the $1,500 robot kits, while other schools bought multiple kits and built prototypes. But their robot performed well, outscoring other schools' robots in one–on–one games of shooting baskets. Health High's robot placed nineteenth out of forty-four schools, higher than any high school in the district, including the elite exam school. Martin, who had left the competition after the games were over, soon received a cell phone call from students screaming, "Miss, we won! We won!" The team received a Judges Award for the team with the most potential. Martin noted the importance of the event: "There's not a culture here yet of valuing academic achievement. We have our failing kids do it for extra credit. Other schools have their nerds doing it. The kids loved the competition. None of them had ever been to a competition for anything. Being on the robotics team helped build kids' confidence, and beating other schools showed them that they can compete with kids they don't even usually encounter." For the next year, the school planned to buy two kits and have a robotics class as a course option since so many students were interested in robotics after the team's success. Investment: $1,500 in robot kit, teachers' and students' time after school.

These relatively small investments required flexible pots of money that the principals could draw on when they saw an opportunity, as well as time from both students and adults, sometimes within the school day and sometimes after. They also required expertise and personnel power to do things that the principals couldn't do themselves. These small investments helped catalyze shifts in hope that rippled through the schools.

CLASS SIZE

Alice Morrison, the writing coach funded by external dollars and partnerships, had her own opinion of what was most important for making a difference for students—class size. The average size of regular education core academic classes at Tech High was 21 and at Health High was 20. By most standards, these class sizes were relatively small, particularly for public high schools. So why did that feel too big to the writing coach? In part because those class sizes were averages, and classes ranged from 14 to 31 students. But for the coach, the real reason was the level of student need, which she felt necessitated one-on-one work with students.

Tech High and Health High, like most schools, didn't have the resources to have an adult sit down with each student individually for all their classes, but did have plenty of students who weren't thriving in a twenty-person class and teachers who thought the classes were still too big. How do you think about class size strategically? Is the money it will cost to reduce class size worth the trust and other outcomes it might yield? If you choose not to reduce class size, can you articulate a rationale for how you're using resources instead?

There are several decisions to make about class size:

- What size classes do we want? Why? What's our theory?
- Will class size vary by grade level, subject, or student need?
- What are the regulatory constraints? (e.g., special education requirements and union contract stipulations)
- Are there ways to use flexible groupings or other strategies to get a "small" feel?

- Are dollars best invested in class size, in other areas, or some balance?

Hobbs and Martin started off with the premise that they wanted class sizes as small as possible because they thought teachers would be able to provide more attention and build stronger relationships with students in smaller classes, which would lead to better student outcomes. Both wanted to have smaller class sizes in English and math, but the only way they had enough teachers to do this was through inclusion—having both a regular education and special education teacher in a classroom at the same time. Even though there were 28 students in the room, there were 2 teachers for a class size of 14. The math teachers at both schools resisted this approach and ended up with average class sizes of 22–24 students with 1 teacher, while the English/humanities teachers had lower class sizes, particularly in the ninth grade, with average class sizes of 15–16. The union contract stipulated the classes could not exceed 31, which was only a constraint when Martin wanted to make some of the noncore classes like PE very large to offset smaller classes elsewhere. Bigger constraints were the special education and English–language learning regulations, which stated a maximum of 10 students per teacher in special education classes and 20 students per teacher in ELL classes.

Both principals used some of their specialist teachers to try to provide extra help on a floating basis across classes, had low overall teacher loads, and had advisories to support a small feel, but did not use other sorts of groupings. Martin made the decision that she was willing to trade off highly variable class sizes (one teacher might teach 3 sections of a course with 15, 22, and 28 students in the sections) for common planning time. Constrained by the school's small size, she couldn't arrange for content area teachers to be free at the same time unless some classes were very small and some were very large. She decided that teachers meeting together would do more for the quality of their teaching than evening out class sizes. When teachers invoked their contractual right to only meet for 40 minutes at a time, this decision looked less good to Martin, but she persisted with common planning time and variable class sizes in the second year.

Both Martin and Hobbs were somewhat strategic about class size, given that they were staffed at the district level of twenty-eight students to a teacher and managed to have much lower average class sizes. They were able to do this in large part by using their special programs (SPED and ELL) teachers, who were staffed at a much smaller class size, in combination with their regular education teachers. And yet Alice Morrison, the writing coach, felt the classes were too big, and teachers and parents in many schools often clamor for smaller class sizes. Why? Morrison described the students as very needy, especially emotionally: "You need everyone to feel safe. Without safety, there's no risk. Without risk, there's no learning." If you considered conventional measures of student need such as poverty, English proficiency, and disabilities, a class size of twenty felt more like thirty students, and that wasn't even counting students' current literacy and math skill level, history of failure, or measures of their emotional need in the weighting.

As with the resources of people and time, Principals Martin and Hobbs faced challenges when trying to use money wisely. A principal challenge was the limited flexibility they had to make decisions about how to use money. Looking at what they did with what they had, particularly the funds from external sources such as the Gates Foundation, offers some sense of the possibilities within constraints and the importance of flexibility in meeting a school's needs. Another challenge was knowing how best to spend what money they did control. Martin and Hobbs had different approaches that came out of their fundamental beliefs, theories of action, and experiences. Hobbs took a more collaborative approach than Martin at Health High and focused on working with what he had. Martin focused on implementing her vision and supplementing what she had to achieve that vision. At both schools, the important investments in the first year were not the most expensive ones, but the ones that aligned with their vision and cultivated hope.

CHAPTER SIX

—■—■—■—

Resource Use
at the District Level

"Small is not beautiful unless you take advantage of
what it can do."
—Jack Williams, Superintendent of
Metro Public Schools District

ech High and Health High did not operate in a vacuum. They were
part of a district, and the district made many decisions that affected
them. It was the district that had the vision for the new small high
schools long before any of the people in the schools had that vision. The
district charged the schools with doing things differently to support high
achievement for students, and chose principals to lead the charge. But
it quickly became clear that the demands flowed two ways. The new
small high schools put pressure on the district's capacity to individualize within a coherent improvement strategy and system. How would the
district respond? What was the district's role in supporting the schools?

Over the course of the last year at Darby Comprehensive High School
and the first year of Tech High and Health High, what emerged was
the need for a district role similar to the one it wanted for its schools.
The idea of "small" applied to the district, too, and was not so much
about size—Metro Public Schools District was a fairly large district—

but about approach. Thinking and acting "small" required strategy, precision, personalization, and relationships.

This chapter examines the resource decisions and challenges districts face in supporting schools, and how they can address these using a "small" framework, regardless of the size of the district. While this chapter focuses primarily on the role of districts and central office staff, the principal lessons of operating "small" also apply to policymakers and external partners who want to support schools.

STRATEGY

Metro Public Schools District personnel told small schools to have small class sizes, block scheduling, humanities, advisory, coaches, and common planning time, all defensible resource strategies. Yet, the district staffed schools using a formula based on a 28-student class size, offered little technical assistance in scheduling, assigned coaches with no needs assessment or input from principals, did not adjust the district professional development model to work in blocks, and provided no extra funds or time for professional development in teaching in a block, advisory, or humanities, all of which were new to teachers. In short, the district did not change its own use of resources to support schools in using their resources differently, which put tremendous pressure on school leaders to manage that disconnect while starting schools and trying to change the core practices and beliefs of the adults and students in their buildings. How can districts support strategic organization and use of resources, particularly when they demand it from their schools? Three focal points in the area of strategy are: vision, alignment, and constraints.

Vision

Like school leaders, district leaders need to consider and articulate their vision and theory of action. Why small schools? What outcomes are we seeking? How do we expect small schools to lead to those outcomes? What does the district need to do to support those outcomes? What does the district need to understand about resources to help schools as they make trade-offs? In Metro Public Schools District, small schools were supposed to be the antidote to high schools' low performance on state tests, high dropout rates, and low college-going rates. However, many educators within the district, particularly those at the failing schools, didn't think they needed an antidote. It wasn't the *school* that was sick. The school was doing well with what it had to work with, namely high-poverty students who entered high school well below grade level in reading and math. Additionally, it seemed like the magic medicine of the "small school" was not being applied to the sickest schools. Darby Comprehensive High School, the school that became four small schools that included Tech High and Health High, had the highest college-going rates and the second highest state test scores of the district's nonselective high schools. And yet the district decided to—in the words of DCHS's principal—"dismantle" Darby and leave other high schools intact. Why?

The superintendent and other district leaders decided which schools would become small schools not simply on the basis of existing outcomes, but also on the basis of their assessment of what needed to happen at the schools to get markedly better outcomes. Their assessment of Darby was that people there were content with the way things were, while at other schools there was some consensus about action around improvement. Something major would have to happen at Darby to change the status quo, which district leaders did not think was good enough. The other district comprehensive high school that converted to small schools the same year as Darby was different—people there weren't content with the status quo and had been working on improvement, but they weren't getting any traction. District leaders hoped small schools would let the educators in that building try some new things. Most educators at that high school saw the need for change, while most educators at Darby didn't. For one comprehensive high school, small schools were a kind of shock therapy; for the other, they were a rebirth.

A primary way the district communicated its vision for small schools was in describing how the schools would look and what kinds of things might be different, like block scheduling and advisory. A challenge the district faced was that the vision many school-based educators heard was all about structures. While Jack Williams, the superintendent, said that structures were a "means, not an end," many school-based educators acted like the structures were the end, particularly because the district made clear it expected to see particular structures in the small schools.

For districts, the question is: How do you make sure a vision is shared and help people imagine what it would look like to implement that vision, but still leave room for interpretation of the implementation?

An example of this issue in MPSD was themes. The district told the teams designing the small schools that each school needed to be organized around a theme. There was no dissension about this, and each school did so. But some themes were much more expensive than other themes (e.g., technology versus public service), and cost was not part of the discussion in the design process, the selection process, or the district-level allocation of resources. Principal Martin at Health High wondered if the themes were feasible and worth it: "Would it have been more honest to say, just do a small school and be about good education, and forget about the themes, or acknowledge that even with the Gates money, it's pretty hard to do this work with the budgets we're given?" Without the Gates money and the donation of the EMT instructor's time, Health High would have had no health courses. As it was, they only had one EMT course, which Martin felt was insufficient for a health theme. There were two main issues with themes. First, both Martin and Hobbs noted that their themes needed extra resources to be done well, and that didn't seem to factor into the district's decisions about which themes should be supported or be accompanied by extra district support. Second, the theory about why themes were important and how they were supposed to lead to improved outcomes didn't seem to be shared. All the district's small schools had some kind of theme, versus Martin's idea of "just do a small school and be about good education." It wasn't clear to the school-based educators why MPSD small schools had to have themes and whether the district had considered or would consider another model. Additionally, the vision for themes wasn't shared at the school level: Martin's teachers thought a health theme meant Weight Watchers and wellness classes, while Martin thought it meant rigorous science and technology preparation.

Alignment

Another strategic decision districts make is about aligning demands with support and accountability. In what order does the district make decisions that affect schools? In what order does the district ask for things from schools? What kinds of support does the district need to supply in order for schools to be able to meet demands? Districts face many constraints in this arena, such as external budget deadlines, but can still make decisions that support good decisionmaking at the school level.

In MPSD, the school improvement planning process exemplified the dilemmas the district faced. Each school in the district was supposed to have a School Improvement Plan (SIP). The plan was a state requirement, but the district had required the plans even before the state adopted them as part of No Child Left Behind. Ideally, the district would have liked schools to write their SIPs after the whole faculty (and possibly some parents) had engaged in conversations about the school's strengths and needs and had collectively decided where to focus their improvement efforts. These conversations should be based on multiple data sources, and the SIP should drive the school's decisions about budgeting and staffing for the following year.

In practice, the process didn't work so smoothly. The district had to have its budget in to the school board by the first week of February so that the school board could vote on it in time to meet the city's deadlines. That meant that by January, each school's budget and staffing needed to be finalized for the following school year. State test results for the previous school year were available in October or November, as were initial district formative assessments. Thus, at best, a school was making budgeting and staffing decisions for the next year based on test results from last year and a little current-year information. The SIP process used to happen at the end of the year, long after budgeting and staffing decisions had been made. Now, the district had aligned the SIP process with the budgeting and staffing process and made the SIP a two-year document.

Tech High and Health High opened in the middle of the two-year SIP cycle. In mid-November, the district told them they needed to have a SIP, and that the plan should be done by mid-January. For Principal Martin, this district decree seemed unrealistic and pointless given the start-up state of things at her school:

> That's foolishness. Total and utter foolishness. And I said that, which didn't win me any points. I actually got yelled at. Like I wasn't in favor

of strategic planning. I was like 'C'mon folks, give me a break. You're telling me this in the middle of November, right before Thanksgiving, Christmas break is coming up, my budget's due, and January 15 you want a SIP? You've got to be kidding. We barely have school rules. We barely have our discipline system. I still don't know how I'm handling attendance problems. My teachers are a mess about grading policies. We've got operational issues that completely consume us in terms of trying to get people to work together. And you now want me to do a SIP in two months?'

The district, quite rightly, was trying to align the SIP process with the budgeting and staffing process, but overlooked the fact that the new schools were in no position to do strategic planning two and a half months into their first year. The issue wasn't one of shared vision—Martin valued strategic plans from her previous work experience. In fact, her vision for what a strategic plan could be and what it took to get a good one made her even more resistant to complying with the district's demand that Health High do a SIP: "Even if I was a high-functioning school, that would have been asking a lot, but I'm not a high-functioning school. So now they gave me an extension until January 30. It's a joke. And I get very tempted to just not do it, and just say, 'Fire me. I don't know what to tell you. I'm working 80 hours a week, and this isn't even on the page of things that need to get done.' "

The extension missed the point, which was that the schools were, as Martin said, "consumed" by operational issues. Martin thought the schools should have a full year to get the operational issues under control and implement things that had emerged from the design planning process, and then they could see what was working and what needed improving. She also had no data on which to base "improvement." Both principals invested some of their limited faculty meeting time into SIP discussions, but neither had a SIP by the end of the year. Thus, the SIP consumed time and energy that might have been better spent on other things, like figuring out what was happening with attendance. It was also a missed opportunity for building trust between the district and the principals. The principals did not hear the two-week extension as a message of respectful listening and response.

Constraints

Another challenge for districts in supporting schools is multiple constraints, such as tradition, the teachers' union, external budgeting timelines, and operational issues such as transportation. A question for districts is: What constraints will hinder schools' ability to organize and operate strategically, and what can we do to help address those constraints? An initial constraint in MPSD was that the district saw the need for change in the high schools, but the teachers' union and many teachers did not share that vision. To address this issue, rather than simply to repeat its earlier practice of telling large high schools that they would be turned into small schools and opening new small schools with little input from the large high schools' faculty, the district decided to involve faculty in the conversation with a goal of what Superintendent Williams called more "ownership" in the process.

Large high schools were still told that they would become small schools, but faculty were invited to join teams that would design the new small schools. Not all the designs would be chosen by the district, thereby introducing some competition and incentives for doing a good job with the design. Design teams consisted of about twenty people, including administrators, teachers, students, parents, and community members. The teams met for many hours, producing thirty-page documents that outlined their visions for the school, including the schedule, how the theme would be integrated, etc. The Health High design team summarized the process at the beginning of their proposal: "The Health High design team has worked together at fourteen-plus meetings over the past five months in a gratifying process that has created ownership for the school and an understanding of the small school concept." As part of that ownership and understanding, teachers expected to teach in the school they designed. Once the designs were chosen, teachers ranked their preference for which school they wanted to teach in. One small problem arose. The union thought seniority trumped design team–membership in deciding who got to go to which school. Since an exception to the union's typical seniority rules had not been negotiated ahead of time, union rules prevailed, and teacher slots were filled with more senior teachers getting their first choice and design team members only getting preference if there were open slots after all the senior teachers had selected a school. So much for ownership. Not only were the principals left with faculties they didn't choose, they were left with faculties who didn't necessarily want to be at the school where they ended up and felt that their time, energy, and ideas had been wasted in the process of becoming small schools. That wasn't setting up the new small schools for success; it was setting up a scenario where more resources needed to be invested in the first year to address the fall-out from the design process.

PRECISION

Precision matters much more in small schools than in large ones because small schools have less wiggle room with budget, staffing, and scheduling to absorb changes. This is a challenge for districts, particularly those with mobile student populations. To support small schools, districts must balance student assignment, staffing, and budgeting to maximize the schools' ability to be flexible. From the schools' perspective, ideally the district would be very precise about student assignment and less precise about staffing and budgeting. This would maximize flexibility for the schools because they would know which students they were serving, and have some leeway with staff and funds. Or, if the district were going to be precise about everything, then the schools would want the district to be strategic about assigning special populations of students and give the schools a little more staffing and budgeting per pupil to accommodate the rigidity imposed by small size. Tech High and Health High illustrate these challenges.

Student assignment was difficult for both schools. At Tech High, Principal Hobbs had trouble building the schedule the summer before school opened because he had 50 more students on his assignment list than he had slots or teachers for. Fifty students wouldn't be a problem in a school of 1,200 students, but in a school of 380 students, 50 students were hard to absorb, particularly when he was staffed for 380 students and he didn't know which 50 students wouldn't show up. The margin of error needed to be reduced in proportion to the size of the school, and even then, it was tough for schools. Health High received 20 more students than expected, less than 10 percent of its projected enrollment of 300. There were enough teachers, though some classes were quite large because the students were mostly ninth graders, but there weren't enough laptops. The school had 305 laptops, 1 for each student and a few spares for breakdowns. The school needed 20 more laptops and the students came with no additional funding that would support laptops.

From the district's perspective, students had to go somewhere. The district didn't want schools underenrolled because with staffing already fixed, underenrollment would mean higher cost. And a margin of error below 10 percent seemed very precise, considering that far more than 10 percent of high school students didn't show up on the first day of school, or relocated from one school to another. Human Resources staff member Patrick Walsh described internal policies as a challenge for the district: "We do things so early, we have to be good at projecting—otherwise, you get upset people and start on a bad note. . . . As a district, we spend money fighting things that we in some ways create." He pointed out that there were nonmonetary costs as well. If teachers grieved a situation that hadn't been projected well, it cost the district money to respond to the grievance. But more important, it cost the district time, energy, and trust: "The contract is an agreement, and a grievance sets up an uncomfortable feeling in a school—'I could be next' or 'us against them.' We can't do it that way. That won't make successful schools for kids." For him, precision was tied to cultivating the conditions for success.

One possible solution to this tension between schools' and districts' realities would be for a district to have a portfolio of high schools in which there were some larger schools that had more flexibility with their resources and could absorb more students or less precision in student assignment. MPSD did have such a portfolio, but didn't seem to have a different strategy for student assignment and staffing at small schools versus large ones.

Special populations present a particular challenge in student assignment at small schools, as well as an opportunity to build in some flexibility for the schools. Both Principal Hobbs and Principal Martin felt that if students had a particular need, the schools could serve the students better if there were several students with the same need. So, for example, Tech High had sixty-three English-language learners, almost all of whom spoke Spanish as their native language. The school had a special program for the students, including separate classes for students based on their English language level. At Health High, in contrast, there were only nine English-language learners, spread across different grades and English language levels, which meant the ELL teachers either had to serve multiple grades and language levels in the same classroom, or students were included in regular education classes and received some inclass support from the ELL teachers. Similarly, with students with disabilities it mattered quite a bit what the students' particular disabilities were, and both schools preferred to have multiple students with the same disability rather than a few students with one disability and a few students with another disability. With special populations, "precision" meant assigning enough students with a particular classification so that the school could consolidate resources to serve them well rather than spread a single teacher across multiple grade levels and content areas. It also meant that the district would drill down beyond the overall classification of "SPED" or "ELL" and look at the students' particular needs, and would assign students accordingly.

Questions districts face include: Can we concentrate special programs in particular schools? How do we balance that concentration with choice for students in those special programs? At Health High, there were so few ELL students that the district removed the two ELL teachers from the school for Year 2 and reassigned the ELL students to a school that had an ELL program. Most of the students and their families refused to move to another school, choosing to remain at Health High and sign away their right to services. From the district's perspective, concentrating ELL services in particular schools was a much more strategic use of resources. From Principal Martin's perspective, she understood the decision at the big-picture level, but now had students with needs for which there were no services.

Staffing in MPSD was done as a ratio of students to teachers (twenty-eight students for every regular education teacher at the high school level; smaller ratios for students with disabilities and ELL students). To maximize cost efficiency, the district wanted to maximize the number of students per teacher. Special programs in particular usually did not maximize the students per teacher, which actually helped both schools by making their schedules possible. Both schools had more special programs teachers than they really needed to serve their students, and at both schools, those teachers taught some regular education classes as well. The schedule wouldn't have worked without a little latitude on the special programs staffing. Thus, in some ways, the district provided flexibility to schools through special programs staffing, though there was no evidence that this tactic was intentional or was the most cost-effective way to provide flexibility to the schools. Patrick Walsh, a Human Resources staff member, said that if he could have, he would have given the small schools two extra positions to help them succeed.

In MPSD, nonteaching positions were allotted either based on total number of students (e.g., assistant principals), or were fixed regardless of number of students (e.g., full-time principal, part-time librarian). These types of positions necessarily cost more per pupil in smaller schools (e.g., Principal Martin's salary, spread across 300 students, cost more per pupil than did Principal Hobbs's salary, spread across 380 students, and both salaries cost far more per pupil than the principal's salary had cost at Darby, spread over 1,300 students). The district recognized these inefficiencies of size when moving to small schools, and even though it proclaimed that small schools could be done on a "cost neutral" basis, it did not staff schools in a cost neutral way (to the small schools' advantage).

While the small schools welcomed these extra resources, some district staffing decisions were puzzling. Positions shared across the four schools, such as the librarian, were allotted by the district, sometimes divided evenly, and sometimes distributed by size. Most perplexing to the schools was that in Year 1, some positions were divided .2, .2, .3, .3 across the four schools' budgets, and then in Year 2, the distribution was changed to .3, .3, .2, .2 across the four schools to compensate for the inequity in Year 1. Tech High went from .3 to .2 and Health High went from .2 to .3, which meant that Tech High gained money in its budget in Year 2 and Health High lost money. This struck Principal Martin as very unfair because she didn't want that position anyway and because in the first year, "the district made sure each school had what they needed," which was not true in the second year. At the district level, the correction was the equitable thing to do, but at the school level, it felt like a loss of money to Martin. It was not clear why the position wasn't spread .25 across the schools to begin with.

The budget raised additional issues related to precision. The district was constrained by the external timeline for the budget and by the budget's sheer size and complexity, which led to some lack of precision that benefited both Tech High and Health High. When budgeting, the district used average teacher salaries rather than actual salaries. This meant, for example, that a math teacher appeared on high schools' budgets as costing $65,000 (not including benefits), regardless of whether the teacher's actual salary was $40,000 or $80,000 (as determined by the contractual salary schedule). The $65,000 represented the average cost of a high school math teacher. Both schools came out ahead under this methodology, with actual salaries exceeding the average salaries figured into their budgets. Due to a high percentage of veteran teachers, Tech High's actual teacher salaries totaled $198,000 more than the average teacher salaries for a ratio of 1.1 (actual to average), and Health High's actual teacher salaries were $65,000 more than average teacher salaries for a ratio of 1.04. A third school in the same building had about the same ratio as Tech High and Health High. Where did the extra money come from? Other schools. The fourth school in the same building had actual teacher salaries a whopping $375,000 *under* the average calculated in the budget for a .76 ratio. The fourth school also had, by all accounts, the neediest student population in the building, and probably could have used the five or six positions that $375,000 would have bought. These equity issues were in tension with the tremendous technical demands of budgeting by actual salaries, which a district budget official described as "unfeasible."

Another example of lack of budgeting precision was in substitute dollars. Schools were required to have substitute teacher dollars in their budgets, but the amount was more per teacher at Tech High than Health High for no apparent reason. Both schools exceeded their substitute budgets, and the difference was picked up by the district. Again, this gave the schools some flexibility because they allocated some of their substitute dollars to other areas and knew that the district would pay if they exceeded their substitute line item. This was one of many ways in which the district supported schools through imprecision—in fact, imprecision was sometimes a deliberate district strategy for supporting schools. With the best intentions, central office personnel sometimes slipped in extra resources when they thought schools needed them, or created situations like substitute dollars, where there was some flexibility in an otherwise fairly inflexible budget. But there were equity issues—why would the district pay more of Health High's substitute budget than Tech High's? Could there be some incentive for not using substitute dollars?

Precision demands technical and human capacity. One possible solution to many of the issues in MPSD would be to go to student-based budgeting, where dollars essentially follow students and students with special needs come with more dollars, based on their needs. Thus, if Health High got twenty extra students, the students would come with extra dollars that could fund laptops or an extra teacher, or both. And if Health High only had nine ELL students, those students would come with some extra dollars that could be used to provide extra support for them (though it would still be more efficient and strategic to assign students with similar needs in larger quantities to the same school). As a technical matter, in a district with high student mobility and a teachers' union contract that makes it hard to move teachers, in September if students don't appear at the schools where they're expected, student-based budgeting poses many challenges. But it may be necessary to assure equity and make sure that students are getting the services they need. On the human side, there need to be decisions about when to be precise and when not to be, for what purpose, and how to balance equity and flexibility across the district. Some schools may have more flexibility as a result of sheer size, and smaller schools may need more flexibility provided through different resource allocation strategies from large schools.

PERSONALIZATION

Perhaps the most difficult task for districts is individualizing within a coherent strategy. One school would like dollars instead of coaches, while another makes good use of coaches and wouldn't know how to spend unallocated money well. One principal needs support in managing the school, while another needs support in mobilizing teachers. Multiple these by the number of schools and school leaders in the district, and it becomes clear that it is a major challenge for the district to understand different strengths, needs, and wants, and to provide appropriate support and accountability. That is the same challenge they ask schools to meet with teachers and students.

Key questions districts face include: How do you personalize within a coherent strategy? How do you make it equitable? The experience of Tech High and Health High within MPSD suggests that districts should customize support, have consistent accountability, and encourage innovation.

Support

Both Principal Martin and Principal Hobbs felt they needed a lot of support in their first year, in part because they were first-year principals, in part because the schools were new, and in part because the job of principal was too big to do alone. They differed, however, in what kind of support they wanted. Martin saw the district as more a hindrance than a help to what she was trying to do (recall her wish to be in a charter school), and thus wanted the district to provide resources and let her have discretion over their use. Hobbs, on the other hand, saw the district as a help in many areas, and generally thought he got help if he picked up the phone and sought it out. He thus wanted the district to identify what resources he needed and provide them.

Two primary functions of a district are to provide services and support more economically than a single school can do, and to create a network of shared ideas so that schools don't have to invent and reinvent everything. These functions do not necessarily mean a district must operate as a monolithic mass, with all schools receiving the same services and support and implementing the same ideas. In practice, no district does operate as a monolithic mass, and different schools do receive different support, both financial and human. The question, though, is whether these differences are intentional and part of a coherent strategy. Often they are the unintended by-product of years of accrued special programs and interventions and unexamined resource allocation.

In most classrooms, there is neither enough time or enough resources to individualize completely. There are some things that can initially be done similarly by all (e.g., learning to take notes), and there are some things that a teacher knows how to do better, but the important learning is for the student to figure out how to do it himself. So it is in districts with schools. The challenge for district leaders, as for teachers, is to figure out what the objective is, what strategies to use to get all schools/students there, where to let struggle and learning happen, and where to provide an answer or at least the tools for finding an answer.

Superintendent Williams thought that the district could have done a better job providing technical support to schools, but that there was also a tension that came with schools accepting technical support. An example he gave was scheduling. A management consulting firm volunteered time to the district to analyze high school schedules. The major takeaway from their analysis was that high schools were building their schedules around electives and filling in with core courses, a practice which was creating problems like students not being able to take Algebra 2 because of their electives. The analysis also looked at the implications of 4-period, 5-period, and 7-period schedules. One of the people who did the analysis provided technical support on scheduling for the district during the transition to small high schools. Yet both Principal Martin and Principal Hobbs thought this person wasn't all that helpful, mostly because he didn't understand their particular needs, so both principals ended up doing their own schedules. Superintendent Williams saw this tendency across schools, with each school wanting to do its own thing, and not recognizing that some things might be generic across schools. It was hard to get schools to look at what was generic *and* what was particular to their school. The district tended to focus on what was generic and the school tended to focus on what was particular—which made sense given their perspectives—and they struggled to find common ground.

This tension between the generic and the particular extended to supporting the school leaders. The district high school reform office provided weekly 4-hour professional development sessions for principals of new small high schools in the months before school opened, and additional sessions visiting small schools outside the district and learning about humanities. Hobbs found the sessions in which district people came "to teach us stuff" much more valuable than the sessions about small schools and humanities because the administrative content was new to him while the small schools content wasn't. Principals with administrative experience in the district but no small school experience had the opposite experience. Hobbs wondered if it would have been better to have individual coaches for each of the principals—who had "totally different needs"—rather than trying to do things as a group.

Another tension for the district was in taking care of things for the schools or letting schools be part of the process. Hobbs noted that the high school reform office was helpful in managing budgets and in doing "go-between stuff" with the district, but that small school principals were often not included in the decisionmaking. Said Hobbs, "They [high school reform] have great ideas about what to do and probably 90 percent of the time they're right, but they go off and do the things and we don't get to be part of the process. And so, even if in the end we would agree, we don't have a chance to learn that." For Hobbs, the issue was not the decisions themselves, which he mostly agreed with, but the process, in which he had not participated. Thus he had lost both voice and an opportunity to learn. This issue of lack of participation in decisionmaking cropped up repeatedly in the small schools throughout the first year. Most often it was not the decision that troubled the schools (though sometimes they were annoyed that, for example, the school with three years of science got more labs than the school with four years of science), but the process of decisionmaking. It was not always clear who was making the decision, why the decision was made, and whether there was an opportunity for the schools to voice their opinion in the process even if they didn't make the final decision. The challenge for districts is: What do schools decide? What does the district decide? Why? When and how are schools involved in decisionmaking? And when do you let schools participate in decisionmaking not because it will be more efficient (which it generally isn't in the short-term), but because they need to be part of the decision to build their knowledge and skills as well as to cultivate trust?

Another challenge for districts is to determine how much you listen to what schools are telling you they need, and how much you have a consistent strategy, like coaching. Especially in the case of new schools, how much latitude and how much opportunity do you give them to demonstrate what they can do? How do you know schools well enough to know where they are and what they need? What central office capacity do you need to know schools in that way?

MPSD provided lots of support to its new small high schools. If anything, it was too much support, or not the right kinds of support, for where the schools were developmentally. The principals had coaches, professional development for several months before the schools opened, and then ongoing support during the year. Martin would have preferred to have money rather than coaches. She found that most of the professional development repeated what she had learned in her principal preparation program, and found that the support during the year conflicted with what her school needed most. Most of the support meetings were scheduled during the school day, in an attempt to not make principals' days even longer than they already were. Martin didn't go to most of the meetings. In October, she expressed astonishment that anyone thought she would go to the meetings: "I just don't understand how people think we can just get up and go at this point in the year. I do prioritize, and I decided that the priority is to be here and be visible. There are crises every day, things we didn't think about." For Martin, in the early stage of the school's opening, being out of the building was far more worrisome than any support could justify.

And then there was the sheer number of meetings. One week, she was supposed to go to a 2:00 meeting about parent coordinators, a 3:00 meeting with the superintendent, a principals' meeting from 10–1, a new principal support group meeting in the morning, and a high school principals' association luncheon. "A luncheon? I don't need a luncheon," said Martin. "I feel a little bad about that because it's not that I'm not a team player, but I've gotta get the team in shape here, and I can't be pulled out." Martin's priority was what was happening in her building.

If she didn't think a meeting would help her with that, she didn't go to the meeting: "I'd rather get in trouble over this [not attending meetings] than not having my building in good shape." For Martin, it helped that she was near the end of her career and would be retiring after being a principal: "It's kind of a luxurious place. . . . I don't have to impress a lot of people. I have to impress my kids, their families, and I have to have results. . . . I have to run a great school. So everything that's on a list that's not related to that means it's not a priority." She had listened to the district talk on teacher evaluations twice, so she didn't go to the meeting for new principals about it. "I can't waste my time," she said. From the district's perspective, new principals needed to know about teacher evaluations—was it okay that Martin didn't go since she had already heard it? Was it okay for her to skip the luncheon with her colleagues? Were there things happening at those meetings that would have helped Martin with her priority of "running a great school"? If so, how to show Martin that the meetings would help her? If not, how to either change the meetings so that they would help her, or spend the time, energy, and human resources on something else that would help her? Or was it okay if it helped some people and not Martin, and if so, could Martin be excused from attending?

Both principals seemed most receptive to support that came just when they needed it, which suggests that part of a district's role is anticipating what support schools will need and then being ready to provide it—either when they ask for it, or by timing it for when they need it most and allowing them to take advantage of it if they find it helpful. There were many examples of MPSD doing this. In late August, Martin received a call at home at 7 PM from Patrick Walsh in Human Resources telling her that he had worked out a September retirement situation so that Martin could hire a teacher now instead of waiting until the end of September. Walsh described his department's attitude as being "we're here to support you." Martin clearly experienced his support that way, describing him as a "straight shooter" and "the only good person in my life," a testament to how helpful he had been in the stressful weeks before school opened.

The following August, the central office had an open house a week and a half before school opened, exactly when principals needed help solving many issues. Principals were strongly encouraged to attend, and all the central office people were available because they knew the principals were coming. Hobbs solved many issues in a much shorter period of time than it normally would have taken him, and described it as "fun." Many of the central office people dressed up for the occasion (Human Resources staff wore formal wear), and principals bumped into and connected with colleagues during one of the most stressful times of year. The open house combined principals' defining their needs, central office meeting those needs, and a spirit of fun and connections, all of which cultivated trust and helped both principals and the central office enact their vision.

Accountability

Support and accountability are the yin-yang of school improvement. Ideally, they are in balance. In practice, however, too often accountability outstrips support (as seen with No Child Left Behind), or support is heaped on with little attention to outcomes, or support and accountability coexist with little connection. For districts, the questions are: What do we hold schools accountable for? How are we communicating our expectations? How do we have high expectations for all schools, and also adjust those expectations based on the developmental trajectory of both the schools and their leaders? How do we match accountability to support? Again, these questions are not so very different from the questions teachers face with their students.

Superintendent Williams saw part of the role of a district as establishing a policy that sets expectations and then holding people accountable for meeting those expectations. He gave the example of closing achievement gaps, which had been a goal of the district for several years. One challenge was getting people to connect their actions with the goal of narrowing the gaps. District-level people discussed coaching and the achievement gap as separate ideas, while Superintendent Williams pushed the question, "What is it about coaching that if we do it one way or another will lead to improved student achievement?" Williams also pushed full-day kindergarten and Advanced Placement courses as initiatives that he saw as connected to closing the achievement gap (early childhood education and more rigorous courses in high school). The challenge was to get other people—both at the central office and the school level —to make the connection.

If they didn't make the connections, policies became disconnected from goals, which meant that people focused on structure rather than content, and silos appeared on the district landscape. An example was the school improvement plan. The district wanted schools to use their data to drive strategic decisions about instructional focus and to align professional development and other resources to that focus. The district communicated this expectation and held schools accountable for completing a school improvement plan. Assistant superintendents reviewed the plans and required revisions if the plans didn't meet their expectations. This accountability had many positive benefits, causing schools to look at their state test data and articulate a focus and a professional development plan. Some schools rebelled against the typical plans and focused on making the document useful for themselves. As long as they could articulate why they had deviated from the typical plan, the assistant superintendents usually accepted their plans. However, there was no accountability for following through on the plan, and therefore at many schools the plan became a compliance exercise that sat on the shelf until it was time to do another one. The new small high schools were another push on the school improvement plans—neither Martin nor Hobbs felt it made sense to write a plan a few months into their first year, yet the district required it. What did the schools do? Devoted some time to it, but never completed it—a predictable, if undesirable, outcome. And no one at the district level asked them why or had a conversation with them about what was happening with their school improvement plans. If they had, they might have agreed with the principals that it didn't make much sense to do SIPs in Year 1.

Innovation

Small high schools were an opportunity for educators to do school in "dramatically different ways," according to Superintendent Williams. When Tech High and Health High did do things in dramatically different ways, however, the district didn't always respond in ways the principals found helpful. The district wanted innovation, but didn't always seem ready to encourage, inspire, and nurture it.

"They pushed the envelope," said Human Resources staff member Patrick Walsh about the new small high school principals. Martin, in particular, pushed new ideas. She wanted laptops for each of her students and an extended day for her ninth graders. She raised extra money for both programs and wanted more support from the district than she received. With the extended day, she ran into difficulties with the bus system—students needed a way to get home after the extended day and the district didn't want to provide a bus. Said Martin, "This is crazy. Every single study shows that ninth-grade students, keeping them in school for a longer day, results in improved academic outcomes. I'm doing something that's not really costing the district any money. All I need is the bus service figured out. For me, it's like you get, for $18,000 [for the late bus], district, you get an extended-day program, as opposed to for $35 or $40,000. And it seems like a good deal. But I don't think the district sees it that way." Martin acknowledged that the late bus would cost the district some money—though it seemed like a bargain to her for what the district was getting. One challenge was that the district didn't necessarily see itself as "getting" an extended day program. Martin also acknowledged that some of the fault was her own—"As a new principal, I didn't know I couldn't have an extended day program unless my kids got bused"—and that she might need to give the district more time to shift bus schedules, perhaps putting in a request in August for schedule changes for the following school year. Hobbs was also interested in changing transportation, especially because the beginning of the school day worked so poorly, with students late every day due to the district's buses. Both principals were told repeatedly by colleagues not to even bother trying to change things like transportation because it wouldn't work. In August of their first year, however, both principals still thought change was possible and refused to give in to the status quo. They both came from nontraditional backgrounds and had a different picture of what was possible, ideal, and necessary. They had a different vision and hopefulness about their own role in reaching that vision. How could the district support innovation and balance that with issues of equity and special treatment?

The issue of providing laptops for every student illustrated that the district wasn't quite ready to support innovation. Principal Hobbs, at a technology school, decided to forego laptops because "it seemed like a mess" to deal with them and "nobody in the district wants us to get laptops." He described the central office technology personnel as having an attitude of "this is what you can't do." Principal Martin, however, pursued the laptops because she felt they were essential to her vision for the school. Her difficulties with the process led her to declare that the district was a "totally dysfunctional organization." She went through the proper district channels to get permission for the laptops and put out bids. The day before she was going to submit an order to the low bidder, the chief operating officer for the district stopped her and told her that the laptop order (750 laptops—Martin's, plus two other small schools' order consolidated to get the best price) had "huge implications for the district," and that they had to have a meeting. Martin was stunned. The order had been approved by several central office personnel, including the technology office. She came to the meeting with her technology plan, her technology coordinator, and research showing that if you don't give laptops to the whole school community, it becomes an equity issue and divides the community based on who gets them and who doesn't. Ultimately, the order was approved after further wrangling over which company would provide the laptops. (The city's biggest vendor hadn't submitted a bid on the assumption that the order wouldn't go through. Once it became clear that the laptops were going to happen, it complained to the mayor's office when the principals didn't accept its belated low bid.)

The process frustrated Martin. First, it wasn't clear whom you needed to talk to about what in the district: "I talked to the people I was supposed to talk to. Everyone said everything was okay. And in the end, somebody who wanted to be involved or was supposed to be involved that I had no way of knowing that they should have been involved—and it frankly isn't my job to make sure they're in the loop. . . . This is not something I did wrong." Second, she felt the district was misidentifying her as rebellious, rather than supporting her innovation: "I was starting to feel that there was an attitude in Central of calling me a renegade. I'm not really a renegade, but I realized you're a renegade if you innovate without having your innovations already be in the plan, the Central plan. Instead of, 'This is so good—one of the first district high schools in the country to give all students laptops, how can we support you?'—they're questioning my competency and saying, 'Well, if you do this, you pay for everything on your own.' " Martin had a clear vision and many ideas about how to reach that vision, but it felt like the district didn't really trust her ideas or her vision unless it matched the district's.

For a district, innovation raises a number of issues: what does it mean for something to already be "in the Central plan"? How do you encourage pushing against the status quo, especially when that pushes on the district, too, and balance that with equity and a coherent strategy? What are your negotiables and nonnegotiables? How do you decide which things are okay for innovation, and what the criteria are for innovation? How do you do that without encouraging the existing perception of favoritism? What would it look like to organize to encourage innovation?

Superintendent Williams said that he was "skittish about only one way of doing things," which is consistent with a personalized approach of multiple means to a common end. The challenge seemed to be that not everyone shared a vision of the "end" and the different ways to get there.

RELATIONSHIPS

Relationships are an essential ingredient in the theory about how small schools are supposed to lead to improved outcomes for students. Here again, districts can support schools through the same principles that schools are supposed to nurture within their walls. Most districts have more than a typical small-school size of 400 students, but few districts have more than 400 principals. It seems both possible and necessary to apply the principle of relationships at the district level, too. Just as teachers need to build relationships with students, and principals need to build relationships with teachers, districts need to build relationships with principals. Superintendent Williams agreed, and noted that he "underestimated" the importance of relationships, which he had once dismissed as "touchy-feely." Now he understood that the process and the level of communication affected outcomes (how people felt about something and how they responded), and that even when people had no real voice in a decision, they didn't mind the decision so much if they understood why the decision had been made and if there were some relationship there. Between the district and Health High and Tech High, three areas surfaced as critical dimensions of relationships: ownership, explanation, and equity.

Ownership

Superintendent Williams thought MPSD had greatly improved the process for turning large schools into small schools. The district's first two forays into creating small schools from large ones had, by all accounts, been unpleasant and contentious, and the effects were still reverberating in some of the schools several years later. The district had pushed the schools hard, telling the large schools that they were converting now, and giving them little time or opportunity to participate in the conversion process. Williams felt that the district's unilateral and somewhat dictatorial approach had been necessary because of the dire need for change and the schools' reluctance to change. But he also thought the district could and had to do better as it took conversion to scale. "We learned our lesson," he said.

This time, for the conversion process, large schools still didn't have a choice about conversion—they were told that next year they would be small schools—but they were invited to participate in deciding what the small schools would look like. Darby was invited to form design teams that would draft plans for the new small schools, a process Superintendent Williams described as giving Darby "autonomy." In the spring, four of the designs were selected to be the new small schools. As the schools became a reality, autonomy and the buy-in process fell apart. First, everyone at the school had assumed that the assistant principal who led the design process would become the principal of the new small school. "We got one out of four," said the Darby principal. To lead the other three schools, Superintendent Williams chose people from outside the school, all of whom would be first-year principals. These principals had applied for positions at particular schools, but the superintendent didn't necessarily appoint them to the schools to which they had applied. Martin had applied to Health High, but Hobbs hadn't applied to Tech High.

Principal selection raised a number of issues: (1) The assistant principals and many of the teachers felt they had been misled and that their time and energy had not been rewarded. And they weren't too excited about the new principals, who weren't their first choice, were unknown, and with whom they had no relationship. (2) The principals themselves were at schools that weren't necessarily their first choice (or even their third choice). In most cases, neither side had chosen the other, which put their relationship on rocky ground from the beginning. (3) The principals hadn't been involved in the design process, which meant that they weren't invested in the design and didn't necessarily agree with it.

The problems with the principal selection process were compounded by the issues that arose as teachers chose which school they wanted to work in. From the beginning, it was clear that teachers were going to choose their schools rather than principals choosing teachers. On the face of it, this seemed like a good move for ownership and relationships—teachers, who generally weren't thrilled about the idea of moving from the large school that many of them had worked in for over fifteen years to a new small school, would be able to choose their school, which presumably would make them happier to be there and more invested in the school than if someone else chose them. Additionally, the teachers' union would have balked at anything other than the teachers' choosing schools. Even though this process was less than ideal from the principal's standpoint and from the standpoint of good hiring practices, it seemed to make the best of what was possible in the situation. When seniority prevailed over design team membership, some teachers did not end up in the school they had designed, and more surprising, some teachers no longer wanted to be in the school they had designed. Most of the senior teachers chose to be in the school led by the person who had been an assistant principal at Darby. These teachers preferred someone they knew and trusted to a particular vision or design. In practice, many teachers did end up in the school they had designed, but there was disbelief and distrust all around.

For the DCHS principal, all of these issues were predictable and avoidable—and typical for the district. When he looked at the "dismantling" of Darby into new small schools, he didn't see autonomy. He saw thirty years of tradition and community "being taken away without conversation," a process he called "the highest form of racism—people on high make decisions because they know what's best." Even when he conceded that the new small schools might be doing some good things for kids, he thought that the process of becoming new schools could have been better. Seniority was the union's Golden Rule, and someone at the district should have anticipated the fact that design team teachers wouldn't be able to select their schools automatically. That issue should have been negotiated well in advance, and if it couldn't be worked out, at least teachers would have known the terms of engagement. As for the principals' selection, the DCHS principal made few comments about the process, but noted that the principals should have participated in the design process because the principals quite rightly had a vision for what the schools should be. Now the problem was that their vision didn't match the vision crafted by the people already in the building. The whole thing, in his opinion, was "crazy" and disrespectful.

A veteran teacher at Tech High was less bothered by the process than the product: "I was on the design team, but the school isn't what I designed." The district wanted leaders with new ideas and hope about what students, teachers, and schools could do, and they wanted teachers to have some say over what the schools looked like, but the process ended up not helping—and in many cases hurting and undermining—ownership and relationships. The rough start contributed to the high consumption of time, energy, and resources for relationship-building in the first year.

For districts involved in transforming schools, several questions resonate from MPSD's experience: How do you choose leaders? When? Who chooses? Who's involved in the design/visioning process? What do you need to figure out with the union? How do you push change and improvement while respecting and mining the experience of veterans?

Explanation

Principal Martin felt that some people in the central office supported her through relationships and others didn't. Patrick Walsh, a Human Resources officer, called her at home in the evening to empathize about a difficult staffing issue and to strategize creative ways to solve the issue, which he then followed through on. In contrast, Harold Landry, the head of Budgeting, sent her a form letter outlining her budget for the next year, neither acknowledging nor explaining significant cuts in her budget. "I understand that we have to have cuts sometimes," said Martin, "but a phone call would have been nice, or at least a written explanation of why the cuts were happening." The lack of communication and relationships led to a time-intensive and acrimonious budgeting process.

As it was, Martin wasn't expecting cuts. "I was basically told that if you've got the same number of kids, you should have enough money in your budget to fund the same level of activity. That was the message from the superintendent," said Martin. She had the same number of students, so she expected to have the budget to fund what she had done in her first year. Through a combination of losing her bilingual teachers and an evening out of shared positions across the four small schools, Martin was down $90,000 in her Year 2 budget. Harold Landry told her she had to lose a teacher. Martin refused and didn't turn in the budget because she couldn't turn in a budget that didn't balance. Her school council backed her up, refusing to approve cuts.

Martin went to the district and said, "If you're going to cut a teacher, if that's your solution, then you need to find a new principal next year because I'm not going to do this job." Everyone was quiet. "This is ridiculous," continued Martin. "It's not just cutting a teacher. I cannot do block scheduling with less teachers. It doesn't work." Harold Landry said, "Well, you could switch your schedule." Martin replied, "I'm not switching my schedule. I spent the whole year getting everybody used to block scheduling." Landry said, "You shouldn't have had those bilingual teachers this year. You're in a luxurious situation right now, and it's not fair." Martin replied, "I'm not switching my schedule because the district mistakenly gave me bilingual teachers last year. Spare me, spare me. Luxurious situation. You've got to be kidding me."

The explanation for why she had budget cuts—that she was mistakenly given bilingual teachers last year when she didn't have enough bilingual students to merit having the teachers—came too late in the process for Martin. The district was trying to equalize resources across schools, which made sense as a districtwide policy, but refused to individualize for Health High, or recognize that the proposed solution (changing the schedule) undermined the prior district mandate for block scheduling and the overall goal of relationships and attention for students. The tension was unavoidable since the district staffed schools at a ratio of 28:1 (regular education), even though it wanted small schools to have small class sizes. But as Martin herself said, the whole tenor of the conversation might have been different if it had started with an explanation about *why* there were cuts, and then might have proceeded differently if the district had listened to her explanation of why she couldn't tolerate the cuts, which was not about a personal attachment to a particular teacher, but a logistical inability to run a block schedule, which was a district priority. Instead of trying to problem-solve a messy situation together, Martin and the district ended up on opposing sides, with each seeing the other as an obstacle.

Ultimately, the situation was resolved in a back-and-forth negotiation in which Martin ceded all of her instructional supplies money and didn't fund her share of a buildingwide aide position while the district covered part of the position. She thus didn't have to lose a position. But she felt "nickel and dimed" and had the sense that the district could fund the position if it wanted to without taking all of her instructional supply money and making her life miserable. This sense was confirmed when the full-time ROTC position that the four principals had cut because they couldn't/didn't want to pay for it was reinstated by the district when the chief financial officer "found" money to fund the position. Martin was furious. If the district could "find" the money for the ROTC teacher, who served seventy students across the four schools, why couldn't it find money for her instructional supplies, which would serve her 300 students?

The district proffered no explanation for its actions, which left Martin feeling that the district was inconsistent at best and hypocritical at worst. At the district level, different people were making the various decisions that affected Martin, and few of them were talking either with her or with each other. This led to distrust on all sides, with extra time and energy spent on conversations and feelings of ill will.

Equity

Even though her situation didn't feel "luxurious," when she wasn't upset about the budgeting process, Martin acknowledged that the small high schools received more resources than other schools in the district. She, like principals in the other small schools, had more administrators per pupil than other schools, and had at least one extra teaching position than the staffing formula dictated. As a result, her per pupil spending was higher than that of the large comprehensive high schools in the district. It didn't feel like enough, but it was more than other schools were getting.

Inequitably distributed resources are common in districts, and usually a result of accrued exceptions, programs, and unsystematic decisionmaking—a combination of intentional decisions that eventually result in an unintentionally inequitable system. The real challenge for districts is not so much inequity—there might be perfectly legitimate reasons to put more resources in one school versus another, such as low performance—as identifying the existing inequities, developing a coherent strategy for resource allocation, and implementing that strategy, even when it invariably means some schools will lose resources as resources are redistributed. It's easy to go along with resource reallocation if you're going to get more resources, but much harder to swallow if you're going to lose resources, which is usually the case when a district goes to reallocate resources.

Some districts address the issue of inequity by moving to weighted student budgeting, in which each student is assigned a funding amount based on that student's needs, and the money follows the students. Thus, if a school has more bilingual students this year than last year, the new bilingual students should bring with them extra funding that helps provide services to them. Other districts determine a policy for the level of funding schools get. In this scenario, low-performing schools might get more resources in the form of coaching, or small high schools might get more resources in the form of administrators and teachers. A district could also combine the two strategies. In all of these cases, there is a rationale that is explainable and visible to people, which makes it feel like the decisionmaking is less arbitrary and less about how "squeaky" the wheel is, or about how much the district likes a particular school leader. Even when the district has a rationale, as MPSD usually did, if it's not clear to the people in the system, many people will interpret decisions as evidence of favoritism as opposed to evidence of a coherent strategy. Explanation is key in these circumstances. The district either needs to acknowledge that there are different rules for different schools, and explain why that is the case, or not have different rules for different schools.

Principal Hobbs didn't fret much about equity. In part, he acknowledged, he was on the favorable side of the inequity. He wondered if he'd be so casual if he were in one of the schools that clearly wasn't getting as many resources as his school. But he also didn't want to be part of what he saw as a "culture of hoarding" in the district, which was prevalent even among the new small schools that were generally receiving more resources than other schools. Well before Tech High opened, in the process of dividing resources among the new small schools, Hobbs noticed that teachers and principals were very suspicious about how resources were being allocated and used. There was lots of distrust, especially of "Central," which included the high school reform office. It didn't help that the high school reform office seemed to be rolling in resources—staff had flat-screen monitors, and the office distributed glossy folders with "High School Reform" printed on them at summer workshops. Meanwhile, the schools had old, slow, clunky computers and felt generally underresourced. Hobbs described the culture as people not wanting to be "suckered" (by not getting what they might otherwise), and "if you don't horde for yourself, you won't be taken care of." Hobbs chose not to worry about it. "I may be naïve," he said, "but I trust that everything will work out, and that there will be furniture in the classrooms when school starts. It's my job to make a stink about it if it doesn't happen, but I trust that it's going to happen. It's why they say I'm not scarred yet—hopefully, I won't be." Hobbs trusted that things would work out, not because he had evidence that the district made things work out, but because his world view and experience was generally that things did work out, because he didn't see others' gains as necessarily his loss, and because he believed in systems that allowed for variation while taking care of the whole. Hobbs was an exception in a district where the evidence suggested that things worked out for school leaders who made them work out and where leaders quite rationally saw others' gain as their loss (in a system with a limited set of resources) and valued their individual school over any sense of the system and its purpose. Even though MPSD compared favorably to other districts in terms of resources, within the district, schools compared their level of resources not to other districts but to other schools within the district and to their vision of what they'd like to see and what they thought they needed. In any district where the level of resources doesn't match what people think they need, it becomes all the more important for the district to be transparent about resource decisions. As it turned out, Hobbs was right. There was furniture in the classrooms when school started.

Like all relationships, the relationships between districts and principals needs to be two-way— a district isn't entirely responsible for the relationship. Hobbs nurtured his relationship with the district in many ways—asking for help when he needed it, getting to know central office personnel in many departments by first name, and generally speaking with people in a friendly tone, even when he was frustrated. His relationship with the district was a resource he invested in and drew upon. Martin, who like Hobbs believed in and enacted strong relationships with students, was less invested in relationships with adults, both at her school and at the district level. Martin unwillingly took on the mantle of "renegade" when her ideas bumped up against district policies and procedures. With the district, as with her teachers, Martin strongly wanted her vision to happen, and wanted adults to either help or get out of her way.

Principal Hobbs, who had taught and worked only in small high schools, didn't have a picture in his head of the traditional model of the large comprehensive high school, which he saw as an advantage: "I'm glad I don't, because when an idea comes or a question comes, the first place I look to answer it is with a small school model—how do you individualize things as opposed to systematize things, how do you allow for the exceptions to the rule, as well as having the rule, or how do you give as much conversation to the exceptions as to the rule . . . You can't operate a small school based on rules. You have to operate case-by-case, and you have to have the time to talk with kids about not just the rule, but the intention."

Districts are a resource for schools. Districts' primary role is to support schools, just as principals' primary role is to support teachers, and teachers' primary role is to support students. Districts, usually populated with educators whose first picture is of the large comprehensive high school, can support small schools by doing the very things they ask small schools to do: individualize, allow for exceptions, and talk about the rules as well as the intentions.

—■—■—■—

Conclusion

"You never know which conversation is going to make a difference, so you just have to keep having that conversation."
—*Principal Hobbs, Tech High*

"Next year is going to be great."
—*Principal Martin, Health High*

The work of improvement in schools, particularly urban schools, is
hard. Why is it so hard? Because it's about changing beliefs and
practices, about changing what people believe is possible and helping them be part of making it possible. Such a transformation is costly,
and requires that we invest our people, time, and money wisely if we
are to succeed. And even then, the best, brightest, and most committed
among us will falter if we do not also invest in vision, hope, trust, ideas,
and energy.

SO WHAT?

The first year at Tech High and Health High offers five major lessons
about what school leaders and those who would support them should
keep in mind as they make decisions about resource use that will help
transform teaching and learning:

1. Invest in big wins;
2. Use resources with your "eyes wide open";
3. "Small" is more about approach than size;
4. It doesn't have to be quite so hard; and
5. Invest in vision, hope, trust, ideas, and energy.

Invest in Big Wins

At Health High and Tech High, where neither the adults nor the students shared vision, hope, or trust, investments had big payoffs when they produced evidence of new possibilities. The robotics competition, college applications, and writing contest all showed that students could do more than previously seen, and the writing contest also showed that there was a potential role for teachers in students' success. According to the administrators and teachers at the schools, these relatively minor investments of people, time, and money had more impact on beliefs and practices in the schools than did much more considerable investments such as professional development. The implication was that school leaders should work on getting the "right people on the bus," creating a shared vision, hope, and trust, and generating demand for professional development before investing heavily in instructional improvement. Principals Hobbs and Martin both spoke of building a critical mass of students and teachers who shared their vision to tip the scales away from the status quo. The highly visible "big wins" that helped build that critical mass included students as direct targets of the investment, some measure of performance against others, external feedback about how well students did, and public recognition of success.

Use Resources with Your "Eyes Wide Open"

When Principal Paula Martin said she made resource decisions with her "eyes wide open," she meant that she had purpose and priorities, had an idea about the pros and cons of particular choices, and knew why she chose one strategy over another. She knew what she was getting into and why. She knew that putting common planning time in the schedule would make class size uneven, and she knew why she decided to have common planning time anyway.

An "eyes wide open" approach to resource use is intentional and strategic. In other words, you use resources for a particular purpose, have a theory about how a specific decision will lead to a desired outcome, and you make deliberate trade-offs and decisions appropriate to your particular context. This requires knowledge, skill, and a vision of possible resource use. For Martin, "eyes wide open" also meant that she was on the lookout for evidence about whether the resource use was leading to the outcome she wanted, and whether she was willing to adjust when it looked like her theory wasn't working. When the ninth-grade extended-day program didn't yield the results she wanted, she didn't abandon the extended day for Year 2—she revised it, imbedding the additional time as part of ninth graders' regular schedules, with regular courses happening after 1:30. Leaders who make decisions with their "eyes wide open" recognize that resources are a means, not the end. The goal is not small class size or fifty hours of professional development or even a shared vision—the goal is high-quality instruction and learning—and intentional, strategic use of resources can help meet that goal.

"Small" Is More about Approach than Size[1]

The Metro Public School District turned Darby Comprehensive High School into four small schools in the hope that small size would mean big improvements in student achievement. Size did matter in the first year at Tech High and Health High. Small size made some things easier—like knowing all the teachers and all the students—and some things harder—like scheduling time for teachers to meet during the school day. But "small" is more about approach than size. You can be "small" with a lot of students or "big" with a few students—that is, you can organize for individual attention through low teacher loads, low student loads, long blocks of time, and periods for support and enrichment no matter how many students you have, and you can organize to pay little attention to students and teachers no matter how few of them you have. Another way that "small" feels the same as large is having small structures that contain large comprehensive school practices. The small structure is there, but the accompanying practice is not. There was plenty of evidence at Tech High and Health High that the structure was not enough—having advisory or block scheduling didn't mean that teachers would actually talk with students or engage them in content in a different way. Thinking and acting "small" also applies to the districts, external partners, and policymakers who want to support schools.

It Doesn't Have to Be Quite So Hard

Hard as school improvement is, it doesn't have to be quite so hard. There were lots of things outside the control of Principals Hobbs and Martin that made it harder for them to be effective at Tech High and Health High, and a few that made it easier. At the top of "harder" list were the teachers' union contract and district policies and decisions. Hobbs and Martin managed to do many of the things they wanted to do, but it would have been easier if they could have chosen their teachers, had more time for faculty conversations, had a longer school day for students, had the option of more discretion over their funds, and not been distracted by mandates like the school improvement plan. At the top of the "easier" list were external partnerships, flexible funds, and some district personnel and decisions. It helped to have partners supplying people, time, money, and expertise, particularly when some of the funds were flexible and could be used at the principals' discretion. And it helped when district personnel allotted extra resources to the schools and solved problems with the principals. The work is hard enough—any constraints that make it harder should be examined to see how they can be transformed to help rather than hinder improvement.

Invest in Vision, Hope, Trust, Ideas, and Energy

Finally, part of what made the first year so hard at Tech High and Health High was that the principals were investing their resources precisely in the ways research and common sense would suggest—but people in the schools weren't ready for those investments. The principals needed to help them be ready first. Even for a leader like Hobbs, who saw his job as "helping people—teachers and students—create dreams and visions and then figure out how to make them happen," it wasn't easy to invest first and then persist in cultivating vision, hope, trust, ideas, and energy. Principal Hobbs, reflecting back on the first year at Tech High, said, "I basically gave up from April on." In the summer, with no energy left to invest, he was ready to quit. But after a month off, he realized that it was not teachers' response that was upsetting him as much as his own: "I wasn't trying anymore. . . . [Now I'm] trying to invest my energy in finding ways to keep myself ready for that conversation and also not to have expectations that people are going to really hear it—to go in with the expectation that people may not get any of it, but I'm just going to keep saying it anyway." Hobbs recognized that "it was never as bad" as people not getting any of what he was saying, but now also recognized that it was "never as good as I ideally want it." He laughed as he acknowledged what he had wanted it to be in the first year: "You say this thing and this person's like, 'Oh wow, I've just had an epiphany and thirty years of experience have just gone out the window and now I'm thinking this.' It's really dumb. Regardless, that's how I felt." Hobbs's theory of action—that with conversation, people would have an epiphany and share his vision—didn't work out as he had expected in the first year. In the second year, he didn't abandon conversation, but targeted it differently, focusing particularly on getting teachers to identify something that needed improvement (they chose attendance), a plan for addressing it, and a follow-up that included checking in about how well the plan was working, adjusting the plan, and involving each faculty member in implementing the adjustment. Hobbs wanted to move the conversation to instruction and to attack the deeper issue of many teachers not seeing a need for change, but felt that for now, he was establishing the roots needed to have those conversations.

REASONS TO BE HOPEFUL

There were many early signs that students at Tech High and Health High were experiencing better outcomes than had students at Darby Comprehensive High School. More students were attending school, more were applying to and being accepted to college, and more were passing the state tests. Of these indicators, the last was the most dramatic, with Health High doubling Darby's percentage of students scoring proficient or advanced on both the English language arts and math exams. Tech High was not far behind. Statewide trends did not see such a leap in passing or proficiency rates between 2005 and 2006, and there was nothing to suggest that the 2006 class of sophomores at Tech High and Health High differed significantly from the 2005 class of sophomores at Darby. With limited data and no causal evidence, any conclusions about whether or how Tech High and Health were producing these results are on shaky ground, but the upward direction of results encouraged optimism.

Martin saw "glimmers of hope" in other places. Many kids who had never been readers were now "hooked" on reading. In the spring, visitors from the Gates Foundation asked two students what they liked best about their humanities class. "Oh, we love reading," one of them replied. "Did you always like reading?" asked a Gates visitor. "Oh no, I never read 'til this year," replied one. "Oh no, we hated reading," replied the other. "You know, I've decided that I actually like reading better than TV now. I totally have a lot more control when I'm reading. I get to read and decide and get my own pictures. I've decided I like that. I can stop when I want to stop or I can keep going until I get to the end." These were not good students, not lifelong readers, and they were repeating the eleventh grade. One of them said to the Gates Foundation visitors, "I came in here hating this school. I was really angry that we had to come to a small school. I'm so glad I'm in a small school now."

Martin also took it as a promising sign that students weren't leaving the school. She had only one student choose to go to another school at the end of the year, and several turn down other options, like a school with an entry-exam requirement or a school with English language support services. Her official mobility rate of 15 percent was still far below Darby's rate of 24 percent. In the second year, her teachers noted that "not enough sophomores dropped out," a situation they were pleased about in the abstract, but not too excited about in the resulting reality of class sizes of thirty-one in some classes. With some irony, they called ninth graders staying on for more schooling a "negative consequence of the small school."

Hobbs counted among the biggest successes of the first year "kids really taking pride in being part of the school" and "gaining trust— that's been a lot of the work." Many teachers hadn't had the epiphanies he hoped for, but he thought "it was a good beginning for working together." Alice Morrison, the writing coach, noted big changes with both teachers and students: teachers realized "that kids could do more and that they don't know how to teach composition," and students were "willing to try and realized they could do it." Jocelyn Norris, the assistant principal at Health High, thought there was "definitely additional stuff that needs to happen" but that they had successfully laid a "basic foundation" for students: "You're valued here. We love you. We want to make sure that things go well for you. Your voice will be heard. We're going to try to create rigorous classes for you. We're going to push you in the right direction. We want you to be successful." She thought that by the end of the year, students recognized, "This is a place I want to be, and I'm going to learn here."

The consensus among adults was that the small schools were better for kids, even though adults and even students might not be as "happy" as they were at Darby. One Health High teacher noted that at Darby, he felt "you could move a kid and their two best friends to any school in the district, and they wouldn't flinch." He didn't think the same would be true now because the school was more "responsive" to students, had more "ownership" from students, it was "more like they belonged," and students had "relationships with adults." In short, the small schools were on their way to fulfilling their promise for students.

Students mostly agreed, saying they learned more in their new schools. At the end of the second year, Health High students said, "Teachers expect you to do your best," and "I love this school—teachers help you get to the level you're at now." They noted that there were more college-bound students, more people on the honor roll, and higher scores on the state tests than in their old school, and they liked being part of a school with successes. They also noted that seniors who had graduated came back to the school frequently to visit. Students liked being at the school. They had mostly recovered from their initial dismay at losing Darby Comprehensive High School and recognized that some things they didn't like at first had turned out to be good for them. When one Health High student bemoaned the loss of freedom she had in "the big school," another affirmed that she missed seeing all her friends (who were now spread across the four small schools), but then asserted that seeing friends "is not good because you can't concentrate." Another Health High student said that he "got used to" the extended day in ninth grade, so he now stayed after school for more support as a tenth grader.

Success brought its own challenges, too, including demands for more resources. Students at both schools expressed their desire for SAT preparation. One Tech High student said, "We got prep three days before the test. We weren't prepared. We need to start preparing freshman year. We saw the guidance counselor once as ninth graders. The guidance counselor is focused on seniors instead of beginning to end." A Tech High tenth grader agreed, saying, "I expect to go to college. I'm going to have to find my own way—ain't nobody helping." Tech High students also wanted more technology. Though they wanted sophisticated technology, they would have been pleased to have more than one computer in the room when they were writing their civil rights movement papers. One Tech High teacher framed classroom resources as a sign of respect: "Look at this room. We're in the twenty-first century, and there are not enough tables, chairs, paper, markers, printers, ink. You'll take yourself more seriously if you're in a good environment. You'd get a better response from students if you could say, 'Welcome. I trust you. You're going to do your best. You have everything you need. This is yours.'" She could say, "You're going to do your best" with the existing resources—and she did, frequently—but she didn't think the physical classroom environment supported that expectation: "People are making do with what they have. That's a poverty view. You tend to be creative, but you're limited." What may have seemed good enough for both students and teachers before no longer seemed so.

WHY DON'T WE INVEST IN VISION, HOPE, TRUST, IDEAS, AND ENERGY?

"If there were a test for vision or hope, we'd do it," said a Health High teacher. He explained: It wasn't that vision, hope, trust, ideas, and energy weren't important. But schools weren't held accountable for them—only for test scores, so test scores were what they focused on. He and his colleagues agreed it would be great if they could focus on "building a professional learning community" with students. But they didn't have enough time to do that *and* raise test scores.

The Health High teacher's response highlights three main reasons why smart educators committed to helping kids succeed don't necessarily invest in vision, hope, trust, ideas, and energy: urgency, faith, and evidence. All three are reinforced by strong messages from outside of schools. The first, urgency, is the area that educators hear and worry about the most. The pressure to raise test scores NOW leads many educators to focus directly on what is tested rather than some things that might be related to what is tested (such as believing you could actually do math), or some things that are important, but not tested (how respectful you are to others). The urgency isn't entirely externally imposed, either. Many educators share Principal Martin's outrage at poor student performance on state tests and want better outcomes for students immediately, not in the "ten years" Martin felt it would take her to get all of her teachers to support her vision.

In the urgent context of helping failing students, it takes a giant leap of faith to cultivate roots, rather than to target all resources directly at the wished-for outcome. As with all roots, we don't necessarily see the fruits of our labors as soon as we would like. One of Hobbs's biggest personal learnings from the first year was that it was going to take some people a long time to change—and some might never change—but that fact didn't change his vision and message to them: "If they never ever changed, would I still be saying the same thing? I would be."

One of the reasons it takes so much faith is that we have so little evidence that roots matter. The dearth of evidence is not because we have looked for evidence and haven't found it, but because we either haven't looked, or we've been asking the wrong questions and searching for answers in the wrong ways—viewing resources and organizational change as separate ideas, valuing numbers more than stories, and looking for fruit when there might only be the tiniest sprout of improvement to suggest the bounty that might yet come.

THE NEXT LEVEL OF WORK

This tale of the first year of two small high schools illustrates the complexity of school improvement and the myriad decisions school leaders make about how to use resources to support improvement. But the story raises more questions than it answers. What does the work of improvement look like over time? What is the role of resources in improvement, and how does that role change depending on a school's readiness for change? How do you assess readiness for change, and how do you best respond to it once you've assessed it? If leaders had less knowledge and skill around using resources, how would that influence their decision-making? What level of knowledge and skill do leaders need to make wise decisions about resources, and how do they acquire that knowledge and skill? Are vision, hope, trust, ideas, and energy the roots that matter for other schools? Are there other roots that matter? Do any matter more than others? How do you know? What does it look like to invest strategically in the roots?

These are questions for the practitioners, researchers, and policymakers who care deeply about schools and the people in them. Schools in the midst of improvement, as educators at Tech High noted, are an "experiment." But we have to be careful that the people in them don't feel like "lab rats" and "guinea pigs"—they should feel like scientists. The work is too hard for any of us to figure out alone. We need to recognize the complexity of the work, and together develop a better awareness of the decisions and practices that really support improvement. The more we see it and document it and show it, the more people will believe that improvement is possible and have some ideas about how they can make it happen.

A Health High teacher noted that the first year was a "honeymoon" period. Things were "a bit calmer" in the second year, but not as much better as he expected. He hoped the school was in "the second volume of a trilogy where the dark side gains ground" because that would mean the third volume with the inevitable triumph of good was still to come. Martin captured this sense of hope more simply: "Next year is going to be great."

APPENDIX ONE

—■—■—■—

Resource Indicators for Tech High and Health High, 2005–2006[1]

OVERVIEW

	Tech High	*Health High*	*DCHS ('04–'05)*
Grades	9–12	9–12	9–12
Enrollment	381	301	1310
Enrollment, weighted for student need[1]	536	429	Not available
FTEs	Teachers: 30; Staff: 39	Teachers: 22; Staff: 32	Teachers: 85; Staff: 126
Status	District school	District school	District school
% Free/Reduced Lunch	75%	77%	75%
% Students with disabilities (SWD)	16% (8% resource; 8% self-contained)	21% (13% resource; 8% self-contained)	18%
% ELL	17%	3%	6%
Race/ethnicity	59% black, 27% Hispanic, 12% white, 1% Asian, 1% other	57% black, 29% Hispanic, 12% white, 2% Asian, 1% other	56% black, 29% Hispanic, 13% white, 2% Asian

OUTCOMES

	Tech High	Health High	DCHS ('04–'05)
Average daily student attendance	90%	91%	87%
Average daily staff attendance	95%	93%	96%
Student mobility rate	16%	15%	24%
State test results ELA	2006 Advanced = 1% Proficient = 40% Needs Improve. = 44% Failing = 14%	2006 Advanced = 2% Proficient = 50% Needs Improve. = 44% Failing = 5%	2005 Advanced = 1% Proficient = 26% Needs Improve. = 50% Failing = 23%
State test results Math	2006 Advanced = 11% Proficient = 28% Needs Improve. = 51% Failing = 10%	2006 Advanced = 20% Proficient = 35% Needs Improve. = 29% Failing = 17%	2005 Advanced = 8% Proficient = 18% Needs Improve. = 48% Failing = 25%

PEOPLE

	Tech High	Health High
Average teacher compensation (incl. benefits and stipends)	$83,526	$81,489
Cost per teacher hour (salary/hours)	$69.26	$67.57
% of teachers with ≤3 years experience	13%	18%
% of teachers new to building	17%	31%
$ per teacher spent on professional development (PD) and common planning time (CPT)	$8,013 (w/o CPT); $8,013 (w/CPT)	$9,197 (w/o CPT); $12,310 (w/CPT)
Ratio of teacher FTEs to school-based evaluators	10:1	7:1
Ratio of core teacher FTEs to coaching FTEs	13.5:1	12:1

PEOPLE *(continued)*

	Tech High	Health High
Total yearly teacher hours (non-stipend)	1206	1206
Total yearly teacher instructional hours (% of teacher time)	698 (58%)	720 (60%)
Total yearly teacher admin./prep hours (% of teacher time)	269 (22%)	231 (19%)
Total yearly teacher academic support and enrichment hours	0	0
Total yearly teacher other support and enrichment hours (% of teacher time)	60 (5%)	75 (6%)
Minutes of common planning time (CPT)/week	0	80
Total yearly CPT hours (% of teacher time)	0 (0%)	48 (4%)
Total yearly PD hours (w/o CPT) (% of teacher time)	30 (2%)	24 (2%)
Total yearly non–PD teacher meeting hours (% of teacher time)	21 (2%)	3 (0%)

TIME

	Tech High	Health High[2]
Total yearly student hours (avg.)	1127	1243
Average length of student day	380 minutes (6.33 hours)	419 minutes (6.98 hours): gr. 9 = 500 minutes (8.33 hours); gr. 10–12 = 380 minutes (6.33 hours)
Total yearly student hours 9th grade	1140	1500
% of student time in core academics	62%	61%
% of student time in noncore academics	20%	20%

TIME *(continued)*

	Tech High	Health High[2]
% of student time in individual academic support	0%	5%
% of student time in other support and enrichment	5%	11%
% of student time in maintenance	13%	8%
Requirements	4 yrs. ELA, math; 3 yrs. science, soc. st; 2 yrs. for. lang	4 yrs. ELA, math, science, soc. st; 2 yrs. for. lang
% of 12th graders taking precalculus and calculus	60%	27%
Ratio of teacher time to student time	1.07	1.07
Average class size overall[3] (core and noncore)	20	22
Average class size core academics	21	20
Average class size overall (core and noncore) 9th grade	20	20
Average class size core academics 9th grade	20	18
Average class size in ELA	21	19
Average class size in ELA (9th grade)	16	15
Average class size in math	22	24
Average class size in math (9th grade)	21	24
Average teacher load overall[4] (core and noncore)—semester	62	73
Average teacher load core (semester)	61	61
Average teacher load core (annual)	85	65
% of teachers with more than 1 subject	17%	9%
% of teachers with multiple preps	>1: 67%; >2: 29%	>1: 49%; >2: 19%
Student/staff ratio	10:1	9:1
Student/teacher ratio	13:1	14:1

MONEY

	Tech High	Health High
Total operating budget, fully allocated[5]	$5,267,283	$4,273,091
Per pupil fully allocated (unweighted)	$13,825	$14,196
Per pupil fully allocated (weighted)	$9,833	$9,963
Per pupil—reported on school budget	$5,802	$6,079
Per pupil—on district budget, spent at school	$2,943	$2,808
Per pupil—on district budget, school's share of management and system leadership	$1,087	$1,076
Gen. ed per pupil	$12,047	$12,820
SWD resource per pupil	$20,130	$20,869
SWD self-contained per pupil	$16,685	$13,584
ELL per pupil	$16,689	$22,012
Instruction per pupil	$5,079	$4,730
Operations per pupil	$1,619	$1,592
Pupil services per pupil	$1,416	$1,641
Instructional support/PD per pupil	$940	$1,060
Admin. per pupil	$557	$720
Business services per pupil	$222	$220
% budget controlled by school	36%	48%
Per pupil private/grants	$312 (unweighted); $222 (weighted)	$668 (unweighted); $469 (weighted)
% of weighted per pupil cost privately/grant supported	2%	5%
Per pupil cost per student hour (unweighted)	$12.27	$11.42
Per pupil cost per student hour (weighted)	$8.72	$8.02
% of staff – classroom instruction	77%	68%
% of staff – core academic teachers	61%	60%
% of staff – support and enrichment	3%	5%
% of staff – professional development	4%	5%
% of staff – admin./leadership	10%	13%

—■—■—■—

Designing a Schedule

The schedule embodies the management of time as a resource and is an organizational tool to support the work of the school. Teaching and learning decisions should drive the schedule, not vice versa. Considerations when scheduling include:

- What will the content of the classes be? What will the distribution of core academic and noncore academic classes be?
- How long will classes be?
- How many classes will there be?
- Will the schedule include time for teachers to meet? If so, who will meet and what will the time be used for?

This section examines each of these questions, including the dilemmas that school leaders face.

The first question is about *what* content is to be covered in the schedule. Content is determined in part by state standards and requirements, and in high schools, by district graduation requirements. On top of this baseline, schools decide what content they want to offer, with several areas to consider:

- Requirements
- Interdisciplinary courses
- Literacy
- Acceleration/honors
- Curriculum
- Noncore courses

The first area to consider is *requirements*—what content do students have to take and at what level in which areas do they need to demonstrate proficiency? In schools, content is traditionally represented in courses and proficiency is represented in grades, though some schools use alternative modes and measures such as internships and exhibition assessments. The first question is whether your school will require anything above and beyond the state and district requirements. In the Metro Public School District, high school students were required to take four math courses and pass three. "What kind of stupid message is that to a kid?" Martin asked. "Why are we setting up our kids for this kind of stuff? I just feel like it's wrong." Martin disapproved of the expectation of failure built into the requirement, and pointed out the practical implications: "If kids don't get through calculus, every engineering school [college] in the country is off the table for them."

Both Tech High and Health High required that students pass four math courses. Health High decided to require that students pass four courses in English, math, science, and social studies, far exceeding the district requirements, while Tech High required that students pass four courses in English and math and three in science and social studies, exceeding the district requirements only in math. While these requirements communicated high expectations, they also needed systems built in to support students who struggled to meet those expectations—a dilemma both schools faced. Traditionally, the schedule was set up to allow students to fail a subject and repeat it the next year. At Health High, there was no room for students to fail—they had to pass every core subject every year.

A final issue is whether students need to get to a particular level of content. For example, what level of math is expected from students by the time they complete school? A key question here is what the content actually is —many students take a course called "precalculus," but is it actually precalculus concepts, or is it advanced algebra? The Health High assistant principal noted that "students were taking calculus, but it wasn't really calculus—it was whatever calculus kids could do based on their previous courses." At Tech High, 60 percent of seniors took courses called precalculus and calculus, while at Health High, 27 percent of seniors took courses called precalculus and calculus. Both principals thought this number should be 100 percent.

The next consideration is whether to combine one or more content areas into an *interdisciplinary course*. Interdisciplinary courses have several potential resource benefits, including efficiency in staffing and scheduling and lower numbers of students per teacher. Instead of teaching four math courses, a teacher might teach two math/science courses, giving the teacher 50 students rather than 100. Interdisciplinary courses may also benefit students because content may make more sense when it is presented in an integrated fashion. However, there are trade-offs, such as content expertise and start-up investments. Do the teachers know enough, or can they learn enough, to teach all the content competently? Even if teachers know the content well, what are the start-up costs? Do teachers need to develop the curriculum? What will it take for teachers to learn how to teach the content in a way that is different from the way they've taught it before? Health High and Tech High ran into these challenges when they decided to combine English and social studies into a humanities class. At both high schools, teachers considered themselves either English teachers or social studies teachers, and had no experience teaching "the other subject." At Health High and Tech High, costs included the cost of a coach, teacher stipends to develop the curriculum, and the emotional costs of teachers worrying and feeling incompetent. Many of these expenditures missed the main issue, which was that teachers didn't see the need for humanities—what was wrong with teaching English and social studies separately? Teachers didn't have a vision that included humanities, didn't know what a humanities course would look like, and certainly didn't feel competent to teach it. Resources were targeted at all of these issues, but many teachers remained unconvinced that humanities was an improvement. Health High plunged into humanities in the first year; Tech High waited until the second year and only adopted humanities in grades where teachers felt comfortable, a concession to the lack of trust, vision, and ideas around the subject.

The next consideration is *literacy*—how will it be taught? Elementary schools tend to teach literacy in long blocks of 90–120 minutes, and to emphasize it throughout the day. Once students are in the middle and high school grades, literacy is often relegated to English class for 45–60 minutes. There are two main problems with this approach: (1) Secondary English teachers often see themselves as teachers of literature, not literacy—and in fact, they often have little training in how to teach reading and writing; and (2) The reading and writing demands on students in the secondary grades shift but are no less formidable than in the primary grades. In primary grades, students must learn to translate print to meaning by reading, and meaning to print by writing. In secondary grades, students must continue to do this with more sophisticated texts, but also must rely on texts for information. Tech High and Health High tackled the question of literacy by requiring that English and humanities teachers use a workshop approach, in which they taught reading and writing strategies explicitly, and students practiced these strategies with support from the teacher. They also hired a writing coach to work with teachers and students on writing. In the second year, Tech High worked to develop a writing curriculum for the school. Many secondary schools choose writing as a cross-curricular literacy focal point.

The next consideration is *acceleration/honors*. Will there be an option in the schedule that enables students to extend their learning and level of challenge? If so, how do you provide this option while still holding high expectations for all students, and how do you ensure that resources are equitably distributed? At Health High, Principal Martin wanted all courses to be "honors level," but both she and her assistant principal noted that several students could be more challenged. At Tech High, a few teachers tried to provide an honors option within a course—one teacher had students read an additional novel, do a writing project about the novel, and meet over dinner to discuss the novel—but Principal Hobbs said that the honors option generally didn't work very well. In small schools, it is logistically difficult to have separate classes for accelerated/honors work because there may not be enough students to fill a class, leading to small honors classes that raise equity concerns and strain staffing resources. In trying to raise the bar for all students, the schools struggle with the issue of how to raise the bar as high as students are capable of performing. An interesting corollary is how to fill the slots if the school creates them. In Darby Comprehensive High School there was one calculus class. When DCHS became four small schools, each small school had a calculus class, and by the second year was working to fill the class with students who were truly ready for calculus concepts by having students take precalculus at a local college in the summer. The number of students taking calculus tripled in the first year of the new small high schools, and looked as if it would continue to rise.

Another consideration when deciding what content the schedule will include is the very basis of content—*curriculum*. How developed is it? Have teachers refined it based on assessment data, state standards, student interest, and repeated opportunities to teach it? A challenge in this area is the newness of the curriculum. A common decision is whether teachers develop the curriculum themselves or use an externally-developed curriculum. Trade-offs in this decision include

- trust—teachers are more likely to feel valued as professionals and to "own" a curriculum they have created and are thus more likely to teach it;
- context appropriateness—designing a curriculum themselves gives teachers the opportunity to tailor it to their students perhaps more easily than with an externally developed curriculum;
- time—developing a curriculum takes an enormous amount of time. If time is limited, using an externally-developed curriculum means that time can be spent on figuring out how to best help students learn it; and
- research/experience base—an external curriculum hopefully benefits from being tested and improved based on use in other settings.

Alignment is also an issue—how well does the curriculum align with state and local standards, as well as the school's instructional vision? At Health High and Tech High, the district and the principals wanted math teachers to use a more inquiry-based approach, but the curriculum was traditional and required much individual adaptation (and thus, time) by teachers to transform it to inquiry. Not surprisingly, teachers used the curriculum in front of them. Lack of alignment meant that people defaulted to what they knew how to do. Teachers' capacity to teach the curriculum is another factor. If teachers don't know how to teach the curriculum, time and money will need to be devoted to their learning, and it will take time for them to move from learning to teaching differently. Tech High adopted a new physics curriculum, and the teacher attended trainings about the curriculum, but there were few changes in the physics course in the first year. Principal Hobbs expected there to be more changes in the second year because the teacher was more familiar with the curriculum.

Hobbs specifically chose not to focus too much on curriculum in the first year—"I'm letting that go," he said. "I'm more interested in *how* people teach." That approach was understandable given the small pockets of time Hobbs had to work with teachers on improving instruction, but was riskier in terms of trust because for most of us, scrutiny of how we teach feels more personal than scrutiny of what we teach. Curriculum can be a resource for improving instruction, as well as building vision, trust, and ideas, as Hobbs discovered toward the end of the first year. By the spring, Hobbs noticed that the humanities teachers, who had been meeting to develop a curriculum, "had more of a vision and a sense of why they're meeting than the other teachers do," which he saw as "the first step at creating something that's really different." The focus on curriculum was helping teachers develop a vision, trust about why they were engaged in meetings, and ideas for doing something "really different."

A final consideration is what *noncore* content will be part of students' learning experience. Again, this is partially determined by state and local requirements, such as prescriptions around physical education and health, but many decisions about noncore content are left to the discretion of the school. Traditionally, in K–12 education, students spend more time on and are exposed to a wider range of noncore content and have more choice about that content as they move through school, with limited time, options, and no choice in elementary school and more time, a smorgasbord of options, and many choices in the large, comprehensive high school. Leaders must decide what the noncore options will be, whether students will choose which options to take, and what the ratio of core to noncore courses is. For some leaders, like the principal of Darby Comprehensive High School, numerous noncore course options are critical to engaging students, providing a good education, and preparing students for life beyond high school. He compared the school's wide array of options to "a shopping mall." For other leaders, like Paula Martin of Health High, the core courses are the focal point of engaging students. "I don't know why we can't hook kids to school with hard classes," said Martin. She changed her perspective about the role of courses in her first year as principal. She used to think that school needed to have special, particularly enticing classes to make things interesting and have students want to come to school, but came to believe that the core academic classes should do that. "We just need to have good instruction," she said. Health High's EMT course was demanding and popular, with juniors clamoring to take it and seniors claiming the only reason they came to school was the EMT class. For Martin, this was proof that students could be "hooked to school" with hard classes taught well.

Finding the right balance of students' time is key. With the external pressure of tests, time tends to be disproportionately allocated to subjects that are tested (Stecher and Chun, 2001). Thus many schools have double blocks of literacy and math, and limited time on social studies and science (except when the latter subjects are tested, as science is beginning to be). Core subjects are squeezing out noncore subjects like art, music, technology, and physical education, which are important for students' brains, bodies, and lifelong health. School leaders must be able to articulate which noncore subjects are important and why and how they will contribute to both improved test scores (which there is plenty of evidence to support) and smarter, healthier, happier students.

Sometimes the noncore offerings define the school, as with a particular theme or program, such as arts. Specialized offerings can help focus the school and can draw students, faculty, and partners to the school, but they can also be expensive, difficult to do well, and force other trade-offs in the schedule. Principal Hobbs noted that he received the same per-pupil funding to run a technology school as a principal running a community service school, which had much lower demands in terms of equipment. One of his key considerations in building the schedule was how many technology courses students would be able to take. Hobbs and his faculty really wanted five classes a day in order to offer a range of technology courses. This would have meant five 60-minute periods. But, Hobbs decided that the benefits of 80-minute periods outweighed the more limited options in a four-period schedule. Instead, he semesterized some courses so that students took English and math all year, and all other courses for a semester. This meant that students could take two technology classes each year, but as one tech teacher noted, it also meant that students got less content, as she simply couldn't do as much in one semester of 80-minute blocks as she had been able to do in a full year of 45-minute periods at DCHS.

A trade-off that school leaders often balance with courses that define the school is that these courses sometimes drive the schedule. Courses are more likely to drive the schedule in small schools, which often use part-time teachers to staff noncore courses. Part-time teachers can be an efficient resource strategy, but may only be available at particular times of day, and thus can have undue influence on the schedule.

Further Reading

While this list is by no means comprehensive, the following resources offer rich opportunities to further explore the terrain of resource use and school improvement.

RESOURCE USE

The Strategic School: How to Make the Most of Your School's People, Time, and Money, by Karen Hawley Miles and Stephen Frank (Corwin Press, forthcoming). This book provides guiding principles for resource use as well as many rich examples and tools for using resources strategically, drawn from the authors' extensive work in school districts. I've been urging the authors to finish the book so that I can give it to the principals I work with as a core text about resources. At last, it is in press.

www.educationresourcestrategies.org. Miles and Frank both work for Education Resource Strategies (as a full disclaimer, so do I). The organization's website has a treasure trove of material about resources, including *The Cost of Small High Schools* literature review and the report *Strategic Design*, both of which are referenced in this book. The website includes web-based tools for districts and schools to use for strategic planning and design.

Reallocating Resources: How to Boost Student Achievement Without Asking for More, by Allan Odden and Sarah Archibald (Corwin Press, 2001). This slender volume imbeds discussion of resource use in the context of change. Odden and Archibald lay out a multistep process for shifting resource use that begins with "laying the foundation for change."

VISION, HOPE, TRUST, IDEAS, AND ENERGY

Trust in Schools: A Core Resource for Improvement, by Anthony S. Bryk and Barbara Schneider (Russell Sage Foundation, 2002). This book challenges the notion that trust is not measurable and draws on the authors' research in Chicago elementary schools to show that trust matters for student achievement. The book describes in detail what trust looks like in improving schools, using case studies as illustrations.

Change Leadership: A Practical Guide to Transforming Our Schools, by Tony Wagner, Robert Kegan, Lisa Lahey, Richard W. Lemons, Jude Garnier, Deborah Helsing, Annie Howell, and Harriette Thurber Rasmussen (Jossey-Bass, 2006). Grounded in the authors' years of experience with educators, this book hones in on the challenges of change and offers powerful exercises to assist in overcoming what the authors call our "immunities to change."

The Power of Full Engagement: Managing Energy, Not Time, is the Key to High Performance and Personal Renewal, by Jim Loehr and Tony Schwartz (Free Press, 2003). Though this book is not written specifically for an education audience, it has much to offer by posing energy, not time, as an essential resource. The authors describe four types of energy—physical, emotional, mental, and spiritual—and provide ideas for managing these energies in ways that maximize performance and happiness.

The Power of Protocols: An Educator's Guide to Better Practice, by Joseph P. McDonald, Nancy Mohr, Alan Dichter, and Elizabeth C. McDonald (Teachers College Press, 2007, 2nd ed.). This book has numerous protocols, or ways of organizing and facilitating conversations. The protocols build trust by creating safe places for dialogue, maximize time by structuring time purposively, and support improvement by supporting collaboration. Some of the protocols are also available on the National School Reform Faculty website: http://www.nsrfharmony.org/protocols.html.

Notes

INTRODUCTION

1. I gratefully acknowledge Briana Cummings and Simone Sangster for research assistance in locating and summarizing relevant literature and Karen Hawley Miles for additional suggestions and ongoing conversations about findings from the literature. Portions of the Introduction and Chapter 1 appear in *The Cost of Small High Schools: A Literature Review*, by Miles, City, and Shields (2007).

CHAPTER ONE: RESOURCE USE THAT COUNTS

1. Portions of this section are drawn from *The Cost of Small High Schools: A Literature Review* (Miles, City, & Shields, 2007).
2. This research is consistent with findings from case studies of high-performing high schools (Darling-Hammond, Ancess, and Ort, 2002; Lawrence et al, 2005; Lawrence et al., 2002; Education Development Center, 2005) and a large body of research about professional development in high-performing schools at all grade levels (Flowers, Mertens, & Mulhall, 1999; Fullan, 1993; Glickman, 1993; Hargreaves, 1994; Miles & Darling-Hammond, 1998; Shannon & Bylsma, 2003; Cohen & Hill, 2000).
3. In a recent analysis of fifty-eight empirical studies of block scheduling in high schools, Zapeda and Mayers concluded that block scheduling seemed to increase student grade point averages and improve school climate, but its effects on teacher practices, student achievement, and attendance were inconsistent (2006).
4. There are a few case studies of high-performing high schools that use advisories (e.g., Doran, 2004; Darling-Hammond, Ancess, & Ort, 2002). Bergeson (2003) found that the success of advisories in lowering dropout rates varied and depended on the specifics of the schools and teachers.
5. See, for example, "Chapter 4 : Movement and Learning," in Jensen (2005).

CHAPTER TWO: VISION, HOPE, TRUST, IDEAS, AND ENERGY

1. All salaries in this book include benefits.
2. I thank my father, Charles Lucier, for many conversations about organizational change, including establishing the need for change and people's role in that change.

CHAPTER THREE: PEOPLE

1. Class size is a different number from teacher-student or staff-student ratio for two reasons: (1) teachers teach three out of four periods in a day, so each "class" or group of students needs 1.25 teacher FTEs in a day, and (2) if classes are taught by more than

one person (e.g., a regular education teacher and a special education teacher), a school needs more FTEs in a day for one "class" or group of students. The hypothetical class size of twelve at Tech High assumes that each staff member is individually teaching three periods.

CHAPTER FOUR: TIME

1. The figures for the cost of teachers' time come from the following calculations: Average teacher compensation with benefits ($82,271) divided by total annual teacher hours (1206) = $68/hour. $68 @ 6 hours in a day = $408 per teacher per day. $408 @ 29.91 teacher FTEs = $12,203.
2. The length of the school year for ninth, tenth, and eleventh graders at Tech High and Health High was 1,139 hours. The school year for seniors was 171 days, for a total of 1,082 hours. The weighted average of total hours for all students at Tech High and Health High was 1,127 hours.
3. Tech High students in the upper grades had more noncore courses because they had met their science, social studies, and foreign language requirements.
4. Sixty-one students was the average teacher load for core academics at both Tech High and Health High. This number did not include advisory, which would add thirteen or fourteen students to the load total. This load number represented regular education courses—teachers of special education and English-language learning had much lower loads.

CHAPTER FIVE: MONEY

1. For more information about U.S. education expenditures, see NCES Condition of Education reports: http:/nces.ed.gov/programs/coe/.
2. Includes grants and private monies, which accounted for 2 percent of Tech High's spending and 5 percent of Health High's spending.
3. The adjusted figure incorporates weights based on identified student needs. Weights used were: Special Education resource = 2; Special Education self-contained = 2.75; English-language learner = 1.25; Poverty (Free/Reduced Lunch) = 1.2; and Regular education = 1. These weights were taken from the methodology used in Education Resource Strategies' national study of high-performing small high schools ("Strategic Designs," forthcoming), which was based on an analysis of national spending data. The weights do not intend to capture what should be spent on students with different needs, but what is typically spent. Weighted figures allow for comparison across schools and districts.
4. The percentage of the schools' total operating budget spent on salaries would be lower than 90 percent, but it is not possible to calculate it because district-level data were not available at a level that showed whether the district-level dollars were spent on salaries or other areas.
5. Organization names have been changed for confidentiality.
6. The district paid for one-quarter of the time, leaving one-quarter for the school.

CONCLUSION

1. I am indebted to Karen Hawley Miles and Regis Shields for many conversations about how "small" is more about design than size. For more of Miles's thoughts on this subject, see her forthcoming book with Stephen Frank, *The Strategic School* (Miles & Frank, in press).

APPENDIX ONE

1. Resource indicators and the methodology for calculating them were developed in collaboration with colleagues at Education Resource Strategies, particularly Regis Shields, Nicole Ireland, and Julie Derderian, with guidance from Karen Miles and Stephen Frank. This methodology was also used in a national study of nine small high schools (see Education Resource Strategies, forthcoming, for comparative data).
2. The adjusted figure incorporates weights based on identified student needs. Weights used were: Special Education resource = 2; Special Education self-contained = 2.75; English Language Learner = 1.25; Poverty (Free/Reduced-Price Lunch) = 1.2. Regular education = 1. These weights were taken from the methodology used in Education Resource Strategies' national study of high-performing small high schools (forthcoming), which was based on an analysis of national spending data. Weighted figures allow for comparison across schools and districts.
3. All times shown are averages. Health High times include the extended-day program for ninth graders.
4. Class sizes are for regular education classes.
5. Teacher loads are for regular education teachers. Teacher load numbers do not include advisory. Advisory adds 14 students/teacher at Tech High and 13 students/teacher at Health High.
6. All per pupil numbers weighted, unless otherwise specified. Weights used were: Special Education resource = 2; Special Education self-contained = 2.75; English-language learner = 1.25; Poverty (Free/Reduced-Price Lunch) = 1.2. Regular education = 1. These weights were taken from the methodology used in Education Resource Strategies' national study of high-performing small high schools (forthcoming), which was based on an analysis of national spending data. Weighted figures allow for comparison across schools and districts. "Fully allocated" numbers include school-based budget, district-based funds spent at the school, and the school's share of the district budget (e.g., for the superintendent). All per-pupil numbers are operating costs, or the cost of running schools on a daily basis, and do not include startup costs or long-term capital costs for large building projects.

References

Archibald, S. (2001). *A case study of dramatic resource reallocation to improve student achievement: Harrison Place High School* (CPRE-UW Working Paper). Madison, WI: CPRE-UW .

Argyris, C., & Schön, D. A. (2001). *Theory in practice: Increasing professional effectiveness.* San Francisco: Jossey-Bass.

Bergeson, T. (2003). *Helping students finish high school: Why students drop out and how to help them graduate.* Olympia, WA: Office of Superintendent of Public Instruction.

Black, P., & Wiliam, D. (1998). Inside the black box: Raising standards through classroom assessment. *Phi Delta Kappan, 80,* 139–148.

Bryk, A. S., & Schneider, B. (2002). *Trust in schools: A core resource for improvement.* New York: Russell Sage Foundation.

Center for Collaborative Education. (2001). *How Boston pilot schools use freedom over staffing, budget, and scheduling to meet student needs.* Boston: Author.

Cohen, D. K., & Hill, H. C. (2000). Instructional policy and classroom performance. The mathematics reform in California. *Teachers College Record, 102*(4), 9–26.

Cohen, D. K., & Hill, H. C. (2001). *Learning policy: When state education reform works.* New Haven, CT: Yale University Press.

Collins, J. (2001). *Good to great.* New York: Harper Business.

Darling-Hammond, L., Ancess, J., & Ort, S. W. (2002). Reinventing high school: Outcomes of the Coalition Campus Project. *American Education Research Journal, 39,* 639–673.

Dembo, M. H., & Gibson, S. (1985). Teachers' sense of efficacy: An important factor in school improvement. *The Elementary School Journal, 86,* 173–184.

Deutsch, F. M. (2003). How small classes benefit high school students. *NASSP Bulletin, 87*(635), 35–45.

Doran, T. M. (2004). *A case study of three high achieving urban fringe high schools: Factors and structures that lead to high achievement.* Unpublished thesis, University of Pittsburgh.

Education Development Center. (2005). Inclusive schools: Portraits of excellence. Three high schools where students with and without disabilities succeed. *Mosaic,* 23–26.

Education Resource Strategies. (forthcoming). *Strategic design.* Watertown, MA: Author.

Education Trust. (1999). *Dispelling the myth: High poverty schools exceeding expectations.* Retrieved February 17, 2004, from http://www.seisummit.org/Downloads/aspd/EdTrustdispell.pdf

Elmore, R. F. (2004). *School reform from the inside out: Policy, practice, and performance.* Cambridge, MA: Harvard Education Press.

Feldman, J., López, M. L., & Simon, K. G. (2006). *Choosing small: The essential guide to successful high school conversion.* San Francisco: Jossey-Bass.

Finn, J. D., Gerber, S. B., Achilles, C. M., & Boyd-Zaharias, J. (2001). The enduring effects of small classes. *Teachers College Record, 103,*145–183.

Flowers, N., Mertens, S. B., & Mulhall, P. F. (1999). The impact of teaming: Five research-based outcomes. Research on middle school renewal. *Middle School Journal, 31*(2), 57–60.

Fullan, M. G. (1993). Why teachers must become change agents. *Educational Leadership, 50*(6), 12–17.

Fullan, M. G. (2001). *Leading in a culture of change.* San Francisco: Jossey-Bass.

Glickman, C. D. (1993). *Renewing America's schools: A guide for school-based action.* San Francisco: Jossey-Bass.

Goldhaber, D. D., & Anthony, E. (2003). *Indicators of teacher quality* (ERIC Digest). Washington, DC: U.S. Department of Education.

Goldhaber, D. D., & Brewer, D. J. (1997). Why don't schools and teachers seem to matter? Assessing the impact of unobservables on educational productivity. *Journal of Human Resources, 32,* 505–523.

Goldhaber, D. D., & Brewer, D. J. (1998). When should we reward degrees for teachers? *Phi Delta Kappan, 80,* 134–37.

Goldhaber, D. D., & Brewer, D. J. (2000). Does teacher certification matter? High school teacher certification status and student achievement. *Educational Evaluation and Policy Analysis, 22*(2), 129–45.

Gordon, R., Kane, T. J., & Staiger, D. O. (2006). *Identifying effective teachers using performance on the job.* Washington, DC: Brookings Institution.

Greene, J. P. (2002). *High school graduation rates in the United States.* Washington, DC: Black Alliance for Educational Options.

Grigg, W., Donahue, P., & Dion, G. (2007). *The nation's report card: 12th-grade reading and mathematics 2005* (NCES 2007-468). Washington, DC: U.S. Government Printing Office.

Hallinger, P., & Heck, R. H. (1996). Reassessing the principal's role in school effectiveness: A review of empirical research, 1980–1995. *Educational Administration Quarterly, 32*(1), 5–45.

Hanushek, E. A. (1997). Assessing the effects of school resources on student performance: An update. *Education Evaluation and Policy Analysis, 19,* 141–164.

Hanushek, E. A. (1998). *The evidence on class size.* Rochester, NY: W. Allen Wallis Institute of Political Economy.

Hargreaves, A. (1994). *Changing teachers, changing times: Teachers' work and culture in the postmodern age.* New York: Teachers College Press.

Hawley, W. D. (2002). *The keys to effective schools.* Thousand Oaks, CA: Corwin Press.

Haycock, K. (1998). Good teaching matters. *Thinking K–16, 3*(2).

Hedges, L. V., Laine, R. D., & Greenwald, R. (1994). Does money matter ?: A meta-analysis of studies of the effects of differential school inputs on student outcomes. *Educational Researcher, 23*(3), 5–14.

Hock, M. F., Pulvers, K. A., Deshler, D. D., & Schumaker, J. B. (2001). The effects of an after-school tutoring program on the academic performance of at-risk students and students with LD. *Remedial and Special Education, 22*, 172–186.

Holcombe, W. L. (2002). *Teacher professional development and student learning of algebra: Evidence from Texas.* Unpublished thesis, Harvard University.

Jacob, B. A., & Lefgren, L. (2002). *The impact of teacher training on student achievement: Quasi-experimental evidence from school reform efforts in Chicago* (National Bureau of Economic Research Working Paper 8916). Cambridge, MA: Harvard University.

Jacob, B. A., & Lefgren, L. (2005). *Principals as agents: Subjective performance measurement in education* (National Bureau of Economic Research Working Paper 11463). Cambridge, MA: Harvard University .

Jensen, E. (2005). Movement and learning. In E. Jensen, *Teaching with the brain in mind* (2nd ed., ch. 4). Alexandria, VA: Association for Supervision and Curriculum Development.

Ladd, H. F., & Hansen, J. S. (Eds.). (1999). *Making money matter: Financing America's schools.* Washington, DC: National Academy Press.

Lake, R. J., Hill, P. T., O'Toole, L., & Celio, M. (1999). *Making standards work: Active voices, focused learning.* Retrieved June 4, 2004, from http://www.crpe.org/pubs/pdf/Making StandardsWork.pdf

Lawrence, B. K., Abramson, P., Bergsagel, V., Bingler, S., Diamond, B., Greene, T. J., et al. (2005). *Dollars & sense II: Lessons from good, cost-effective small schools.* Cincinnati, OH: KnowledgeWorks Foundation.

Lawrence, B. K., Bingler, S., Diamond, B., Hill, B., Hoffman, J. L., Howley, C. B., et al. (2002). *Dollars & sense: The cost effectiveness of small schools.* Cincinnati, OH: KnowledgeWorks Foundation.

Lee, J., Grigg, W., & Dion, G. (2007). *The nation's report card: Mathematics 2007* (NCES 2007-494). Washington, DC: U.S. Department of Education.

Lee, J., Grigg, W., & Donahue, P. (2007). *The nation's report card: Reading 2007* (NCES 2007-496). Washington, DC: U.S. Department of Education.

Liu, E. (2004). *Information-rich, information-poor: New teachers' experiences of hiring in four states.* Unpublished thesis, Harvard University.

Marchant, G. J., & Paulson, S. B. (2001). Differential school functioning in a block schedule: A comparison of academic profiles. *High School Journal, 84*(4).

Miles, K. H. (2001). *Rethinking school resources.* Retrieved May 11, 2004, from http://www.naschools.org/uploadedfiles/rethinking-resources.pdf

Miles, K. H., City, E. A., & Shields, R. (2007). *The cost of small high schools: A literature review.* Boston: Education Resource Strategies.

Miles, K. H., & Darling-Hammond, L. (1998). Rethinking the allocation of teaching resources: Some lessons from high-performing schools. *Educational Evaluation and Policy Analysis, 20*(1), 9–29.

Miles, K. H., & Frank, S. (in press). *The strategic school: How to make the most of your school's people, time, and money*. Thousand Oaks, CA: Corwin Press.

Miller, R. T. (2006). *The causal impact of teacher absence on student achievement*. Unpublished thesis, Harvard University.

Mishel, L., & Rothstein, R. (Ed.). (2002). *The class size debate*. Washington, DC: Economic Policy Institute.

National Center for Education Statistics. (2005). *Revenues and expenditures for public elementary and secondary education: School year 2002–2003* (NCES 2005-353), Current Expenditures per Student.

Natriello, G. (1984). Teachers' perceptions of the frequency of evaluation and assessments of their effort and effectiveness. *American Educational Research Journal, 21*, 579–595.

Newmann, F. M., Smith, B., Allensworth, E., & Bryk, A. S. (2001). *School instructional program coherence: Benefits and challenges*. Chicago: Chicago Consortium on School Research.

Odden, A., & Archibald, S. (2001). *Reallocating resources: How to boost student achievement without asking for more*. Thousand Oaks, CA: Corwin Press.

OECD. (2004). *Education at a glance 2004*. Table D2.3. http://www.oecd.org/document /11/0,2340,en_2649_201185_33712011_1_1_1_1,00.html

Powell, A. G., Farrar, E., & Cohen, D. K. (1985). *The shopping mall high school: Winners and losers in the educational marketplace*. Boston: Houghton Mifflin.

Resource. (2003). WordNet ® 2.0. Princeton University.

Rice, J., Croninger, R., & Roellke, C. (2002). The effect of block scheduling high school mathematics courses on student achievement and teachers' use of time: Implications for educational productivity. *Economics of Education Review, 21*, 599–607.

Rivkin, S. G., Hanushek, E. A., & Kain, J. F. (2005). Teachers, schools, and academic achievement. *Econometrica, 73*, 417–458.

Rosenholtz, S. J. (1985). Effective schools: Interpreting the evidence. *American Journal of Education, 93*, 352–388.

Sanders, W. L., & Rivers, J. C. (1996). *Cumulative and residual effects of teachers on future student academic achievement*. Knoxville: University of Tennessee Value–Added Research and Assessment Center.

Shannon, G. S., & Bylsma, P. (2003). *Nine characteristics of high-performing schools: A research-based resource for school leadership teams to assist with the School Improvement Process*. Olympia, WA: Office of Superintendent of Public Instruction.

Sizer, T. R. (1984). *Horace's compromise: The dilemma of the American high school*. Boston: Houghton Mifflin.

Springboard Schools. (2003). *After the test: How schools are using data to close the achievement gap*. San Francisco: Author.

Stecher, B., & Chun, T. (2001). *School and classroom practices during two years of education reform in Washington State* (CSE Technical Report 550). Los Angeles: CRESST.

Teacher attrition: A costly loss to the nation and to the states. (2005). Washington, DC: Alliance for Excellent Education.

Thompson, A. M. (1998). *Characteristics of high and low performing high schools in Maine.* Gorham: Maine Education Policy Research Institute.

Tyack, D., & Cuban, L. (1995). *Tinkering toward utopia: A century of public school reform.* Cambridge, MA: Harvard University Press.

Veal, W. R., & Flinders, D. J. (2001). How block scheduling reform affects classroom practice. *High School Journal, 84*(4) .

Wayne, A. J. & Youngs, P. (2003). Teacher characteristics and student achievement gains: A review. *Review of Educational Research, 73*(1), 89–122.

Zapeda, S. J., & Mayers, R. S. (2001). New kids on the block schedule: Beginning teachers face challenges. *High School Journal, 84*(4), 1–11.

Zapeda, S. J., & Mayers, R. S. (2006). An analysis of research on block scheduling. *Review of Educational Research, 76*(1), 137–170.

About the Author

Elizabeth A. City helps educators improve instruction through leadership development and the strategic use of data and resources. She works primarily with urban school districts and is a faculty member at Boston's School Leadership Institute. City has served as a teacher, instructional coach, and principal. She is coeditor of *Data Wise: A Step-by-Step Guide to Using Assessment Results to Improve Teaching and Learning* (Harvard Education Press, 2005) and coauthor of *The Teacher's Guide to Leading Student-Centered Discussions: Talking about Texts in the Classroom* (Corwin Press, 2006).

Index